50 Meal Prep for Athlete Recipes for Home

By: Kelly Johnson

Table of Contents

- Chicken Stir-Fry
- Quinoa Salad with Roasted Vegetables
- Beef and Broccoli
- Mediterranean Chickpea Salad
- Teriyaki Salmon with Brown Rice
- Turkey Meatballs with Marinara Sauce
- Thai Green Curry with Tofu
- Lemon Garlic Shrimp with Zucchini Noodles
- Black Bean and Corn Quesadillas
- Greek Chicken Bowls
- Lentil Soup
- BBQ Pulled Pork Sandwiches
- Caprese Pasta Salad
- Cauliflower Fried Rice
- Moroccan Couscous with Chickpeas
- Teriyaki Chicken Lettuce Wraps
- Spinach and Feta Stuffed Chicken Breast
- Spaghetti Squash Pad Thai
- Chili con Carne
- Sweet Potato and Black Bean Tacos
- Pesto Pasta with Cherry Tomatoes
- Eggplant Parmesan
- Lemon Herb Grilled Chicken
- Mexican Quinoa Stuffed Peppers
- Tuna Salad Lettuce Wraps
- Ratatouille
- Hawaiian Chicken Skewers
- Butternut Squash Soup
- Turkey Chili
- Caprese Stuffed Portobello Mushrooms
- Veggie Frittata
- Beef Kebabs with Chimichurri Sauce
- Buffalo Chicken Wraps
- Mediterranean Orzo Salad
- Baked Cod with Garlic Butter

- Vegan Sloppy Joes
- Roasted Vegetable and Hummus Wraps
- Asian Chicken Lettuce Wraps
- Stuffed Bell Peppers with Quinoa and Ground Turkey
- Lemon Pepper Salmon
- Southwestern Quinoa Salad
- Chicken Enchiladas
- Ratatouille
- Coconut Curry Chicken
- Mediterranean Stuffed Sweet Potatoes
- Beef and Mushroom Stir-Fry
- Shrimp Tacos with Mango Salsa
- Italian Sausage and Peppers
- Cauliflower Tikka Masala
- Greek Salad with Grilled Chicken

Chicken Stir-Fry

Ingredients:

- 1 lb (450g) boneless, skinless chicken breast or thigh, thinly sliced
- 2 cups mixed vegetables (bell peppers, broccoli, snap peas, carrots, etc.), sliced
- 3 cloves garlic, minced
- 1-inch piece of ginger, minced
- 2 tablespoons soy sauce
- 1 tablespoon oyster sauce
- 1 tablespoon hoisin sauce
- 1 tablespoon cornstarch (optional, for thickening the sauce)
- 1 tablespoon vegetable oil
- Salt and pepper, to taste
- Cooked rice or noodles, for serving

Instructions:

1. Prepare the Sauce: In a small bowl, mix together soy sauce, oyster sauce, hoisin sauce, and cornstarch (if using). Set aside.
2. Cook the Chicken: Heat vegetable oil in a large skillet or wok over medium-high heat. Add minced garlic and ginger, stir for 30 seconds until fragrant. Add the sliced chicken and cook until browned and cooked through, about 5-7 minutes. Remove chicken from the skillet and set aside.
3. Stir-Fry Vegetables: In the same skillet or wok, add a bit more oil if needed. Add the mixed vegetables and stir-fry for 3-4 minutes until they are crisp-tender.
4. Combine and Simmer: Return the cooked chicken to the skillet. Pour the sauce over the chicken and vegetables. Stir everything together and let it simmer for 2-3 minutes until the sauce has thickened slightly and everything is heated through.
5. Serve: Serve the chicken stir-fry hot over cooked rice or noodles. Garnish with sliced green onions or sesame seeds if desired.

Enjoy your delicious chicken stir-fry! Adjust the seasonings and vegetables according to your preference for a personalized touch.

Quinoa Salad with Roasted Vegetables

Ingredients:

- 1 cup quinoa
- 2 cups water or vegetable broth
- 1 medium red bell pepper, diced
- 1 medium yellow bell pepper, diced
- 1 small zucchini, diced
- 1 small yellow squash, diced
- 1 red onion, thinly sliced
- 2 tablespoons olive oil
- Salt and pepper, to taste
- 1/2 teaspoon dried thyme (optional)
- 1/2 cup cherry tomatoes, halved
- 1/4 cup chopped fresh parsley or cilantro
- Juice of 1 lemon
- 2 tablespoons balsamic vinegar
- Optional: crumbled feta cheese or goat cheese

Instructions:

1. Preheat Oven: Preheat your oven to 400°F (200°C).
2. Prepare Quinoa: Rinse the quinoa under cold water to remove any bitterness. In a medium saucepan, combine quinoa and water or vegetable broth. Bring to a boil, then reduce heat to low, cover, and simmer for about 15 minutes, or until quinoa is cooked and water is absorbed. Remove from heat and let it sit covered for 5 minutes. Fluff with a fork.
3. Roast Vegetables: While quinoa is cooking, spread diced bell peppers, zucchini, yellow squash, and red onion on a baking sheet. Drizzle with olive oil, sprinkle with salt, pepper, and dried thyme (if using). Toss to coat evenly. Roast in the preheated oven for 20-25 minutes, or until vegetables are tender and slightly caramelized, stirring halfway through.
4. Assemble Salad: In a large bowl, combine cooked quinoa and roasted vegetables. Add cherry tomatoes, chopped parsley or cilantro, lemon juice, and balsamic vinegar. Toss gently to combine all ingredients.
5. Serve: Serve the quinoa salad warm, at room temperature, or chilled. If desired, sprinkle with crumbled feta cheese or goat cheese before serving.
6. Storage: This salad stores well in the refrigerator for up to 3-4 days, making it perfect for meal prep.

Enjoy your hearty and nutritious quinoa salad with roasted vegetables! Adjust the seasoning and vegetables according to your taste preferences and what's in season.

Beef and Broccoli

Ingredients:

- 1 lb (450g) flank steak or sirloin steak, thinly sliced against the grain
- 2 cups broccoli florets
- 2-3 cloves garlic, minced
- 1-inch piece of ginger, minced
- 1/2 cup low-sodium soy sauce
- 1/4 cup oyster sauce
- 2 tablespoons brown sugar or honey
- 1 tablespoon cornstarch
- 1/4 cup water
- 2 tablespoons vegetable oil
- Cooked rice, for serving

Instructions:

1. Prepare the Sauce: In a small bowl, whisk together soy sauce, oyster sauce, brown sugar or honey, cornstarch, and water until smooth. Set aside.
2. Cook the Beef: Heat 1 tablespoon of vegetable oil in a large skillet or wok over medium-high heat. Add the minced garlic and ginger, stir for 30 seconds until fragrant. Add the sliced beef in a single layer and cook for about 2-3 minutes until browned. Remove beef from the skillet and set aside.
3. Stir-Fry the Broccoli: In the same skillet or wok, add another tablespoon of vegetable oil if needed. Add the broccoli florets and stir-fry for about 3-4 minutes until they are crisp-tender. If you prefer softer broccoli, you can cover the skillet for 1-2 minutes to steam them slightly.
4. Combine and Simmer: Return the cooked beef to the skillet. Give the sauce a quick stir and then pour it over the beef and broccoli. Stir everything together and let it simmer for 2-3 minutes until the sauce thickens and coats the beef and broccoli evenly.
5. Serve: Serve the beef and broccoli hot over cooked rice. Optionally, garnish with sliced green onions or sesame seeds for extra flavor and texture.

Enjoy your homemade beef and broccoli stir-fry! It's a delicious and nutritious dish that's perfect for a quick and flavorful meal. Adjust the sauce ingredients to your taste preference for a personalized touch.

Mediterranean Chickpea Salad

Ingredients:

- 2 cups cooked chickpeas (or 1 can, drained and rinsed)
- 1 cup cherry tomatoes, halved
- 1 cucumber, diced
- 1/2 red onion, thinly sliced
- 1/2 cup Kalamata olives, pitted and sliced
- 1/2 cup crumbled feta cheese
- 1/4 cup chopped fresh parsley
- 1/4 cup chopped fresh mint (optional)
- Juice of 1 lemon
- 3 tablespoons extra virgin olive oil
- 1 clove garlic, minced
- 1 teaspoon dried oregano
- Salt and pepper, to taste

Instructions:

1. Prepare the Dressing: In a small bowl, whisk together the lemon juice, extra virgin olive oil, minced garlic, dried oregano, salt, and pepper. Set aside.
2. Assemble the Salad: In a large bowl, combine the cooked chickpeas, halved cherry tomatoes, diced cucumber, thinly sliced red onion, sliced Kalamata olives, crumbled feta cheese, chopped parsley, and chopped mint (if using).
3. Add the Dressing: Pour the dressing over the salad ingredients. Toss gently to combine, ensuring everything is evenly coated with the dressing.
4. Chill and Serve: Refrigerate the salad for at least 30 minutes to allow the flavors to meld together. This salad can be served chilled or at room temperature.
5. Serve: Serve the Mediterranean Chickpea Salad as a side dish or a light main course. It pairs wonderfully with grilled meats or as part of a mezze platter.

Enjoy this Mediterranean-inspired salad with its fresh and vibrant flavors! Adjust the ingredients and seasoning according to your taste preference for a personalized touch.

Teriyaki Salmon with Brown Rice

Ingredients:

- 4 salmon fillets (about 6 oz each), skin-on or skinless
- 1 cup brown rice
- 2 cups water or vegetable broth
- 1/2 cup low-sodium soy sauce
- 1/4 cup water
- 3 tablespoons honey or brown sugar
- 2 tablespoons rice vinegar
- 1 tablespoon cornstarch
- 2 cloves garlic, minced
- 1 teaspoon minced ginger
- 1 tablespoon vegetable oil
- Optional garnish: sliced green onions, sesame seeds

Instructions:

1. Cook Brown Rice: Rinse the brown rice under cold water. In a medium saucepan, combine the brown rice and 2 cups of water or vegetable broth. Bring to a boil, then reduce heat to low, cover, and simmer for about 40-45 minutes, or until rice is tender and water is absorbed. Remove from heat and let it sit covered for 5 minutes. Fluff with a fork.
2. Prepare Teriyaki Sauce: In a small bowl, whisk together soy sauce, 1/4 cup water, honey or brown sugar, rice vinegar, cornstarch, minced garlic, and minced ginger until smooth. Set aside.
3. Cook Salmon: Heat vegetable oil in a large skillet over medium-high heat. If using skin-on salmon, place the salmon fillets in the skillet skin-side down first. Cook for about 4-5 minutes until the skin is crispy and golden. Flip the salmon and cook for another 3-4 minutes until salmon is cooked through and flakes easily with a fork. If using skinless salmon, cook each side for about 4-5 minutes until browned and cooked through.
4. Add Teriyaki Sauce: Once the salmon is cooked, pour the prepared teriyaki sauce into the skillet. Bring the sauce to a simmer and cook for 1-2 minutes, stirring gently, until the sauce thickens slightly and coats the salmon.
5. Serve: Serve the teriyaki salmon hot over the cooked brown rice. Drizzle extra teriyaki sauce from the skillet over the salmon and rice. Garnish with sliced green onions and sesame seeds if desired.

Enjoy your flavorful and nutritious Teriyaki Salmon with Brown Rice! It's a satisfying dish that's perfect for a wholesome meal. Adjust the sweetness and seasoning of the teriyaki sauce according to your taste preference.

Turkey Meatballs with Marinara Sauce

Ingredients:

For the Meatballs:

- 1 lb (450g) ground turkey (preferably lean)
- 1/2 cup breadcrumbs (panko or regular)
- 1/4 cup grated Parmesan cheese
- 1/4 cup milk
- 1 large egg
- 2 cloves garlic, minced
- 2 tablespoons chopped fresh parsley (or 1 tablespoon dried parsley)
- 1/2 teaspoon dried oregano
- 1/2 teaspoon dried basil
- 1/2 teaspoon salt
- 1/4 teaspoon black pepper
- Olive oil, for cooking

For the Marinara Sauce:

- 1 tablespoon olive oil
- 1 small onion, finely chopped
- 2 cloves garlic, minced
- 1 (28 oz / 800g) can crushed tomatoes
- 1 teaspoon dried oregano
- 1 teaspoon dried basil
- Salt and pepper, to taste
- Optional: Red pepper flakes, for heat (if desired)
- Fresh basil or parsley, chopped, for garnish

Instructions:

1. Make the Meatballs:
     - In a large bowl, combine ground turkey, breadcrumbs, grated Parmesan cheese, milk, egg, minced garlic, parsley, oregano, basil, salt, and pepper. Use your hands or a spoon to mix everything together until well combined.
     - Shape the mixture into meatballs, about 1-1.5 inches in diameter, and place them on a plate or baking sheet lined with parchment paper.
2. Cook the Meatballs:
     - Heat a large skillet over medium-high heat and add enough olive oil to coat the bottom of the skillet.
     - Add the meatballs to the skillet in a single layer, making sure not to overcrowd them. Cook for about 3-4 minutes, turning occasionally, until browned on all sides.

- - Remove the meatballs from the skillet and set them aside.
3. Make the Marinara Sauce:
   - In the same skillet, heat 1 tablespoon of olive oil over medium heat. Add finely chopped onion and cook for 3-4 minutes until softened and translucent.
   - Add minced garlic and cook for another 1-2 minutes until fragrant.
   - Pour in the crushed tomatoes and stir to combine. Add dried oregano, dried basil, salt, pepper, and red pepper flakes (if using). Bring the sauce to a simmer.
4. Simmer the Meatballs in Sauce:
   - Return the browned meatballs to the skillet with the marinara sauce. Spoon some of the sauce over the meatballs to coat them evenly.
   - Cover the skillet with a lid and simmer gently for about 15-20 minutes, or until the meatballs are cooked through and the flavors have melded together.
5. Serve:
   - Serve the turkey meatballs hot, spooned over cooked pasta or with crusty bread on the side. Garnish with chopped fresh basil or parsley.

Enjoy your homemade turkey meatballs with marinara sauce! It's a comforting and satisfying dish that's perfect for a family dinner or entertaining guests. Adjust the seasoning and spice level according to your taste preference.

Thai Green Curry with Tofu

Ingredients:

- 1 block (14-16 oz) firm tofu, drained and cut into cubes
- 2 tablespoons vegetable oil
- 1 onion, thinly sliced
- 2 bell peppers (any color), thinly sliced
- 1 zucchini, sliced into half moons
- 1 cup sliced mushrooms (button or cremini)
- 3-4 tablespoons Thai green curry paste (adjust to taste)
- 1 (14 oz) can coconut milk
- 1 cup vegetable broth
- 1 tablespoon soy sauce or tamari
- 1 tablespoon brown sugar or coconut sugar
- Juice of 1 lime
- Salt, to taste
- Fresh basil or cilantro, chopped, for garnish
- Cooked rice or noodles, for serving

Instructions:

1. Prepare the Tofu:
    - Drain the tofu and pat it dry with paper towels. Cut the tofu into cubes and set aside.
2. Sauté the Vegetables:
    - Heat 1 tablespoon of vegetable oil in a large skillet or wok over medium-high heat. Add the sliced onion and bell peppers. Stir-fry for 3-4 minutes until they start to soften.
    - Add the sliced zucchini and mushrooms. Continue to stir-fry for another 2-3 minutes until vegetables are tender-crisp. Remove the vegetables from the skillet and set aside.
3. Cook the Tofu:
    - In the same skillet or wok, add the remaining tablespoon of vegetable oil. Add the tofu cubes in a single layer. Cook for about 4-5 minutes, turning occasionally, until all sides are golden brown and crispy. Remove the tofu from the skillet and set aside.
4. Make the Green Curry Sauce:
    - Reduce the heat to medium. Add Thai green curry paste to the skillet. Stir and cook for about 1 minute until fragrant.
    - Pour in the coconut milk and vegetable broth. Stir to combine, scraping any browned bits from the bottom of the skillet.
    - Add soy sauce or tamari, brown sugar or coconut sugar, and lime juice. Stir well and let the sauce simmer for 5-7 minutes to allow the flavors to meld together. Taste and adjust seasoning with salt if needed.

5. Combine and Simmer:
    - Return the sautéed vegetables and crispy tofu to the skillet with the green curry sauce. Stir gently to coat everything with the sauce.
    - Simmer the curry for another 3-4 minutes, stirring occasionally, until everything is heated through and the sauce has thickened slightly.
6. Serve:
    - Serve the Thai Green Curry with Tofu hot over cooked rice or noodles.
    - Garnish with chopped fresh basil or cilantro.

Enjoy your homemade Thai Green Curry with Tofu! It's a comforting and flavorful dish that's perfect for a satisfying meal. Adjust the spiciness by adding more or less green curry paste according to your preference.

Lemon Garlic Shrimp with Zucchini Noodles

Ingredients:

- 1 lb (450g) large shrimp, peeled and deveined
- 3-4 medium zucchini
- 4 cloves garlic, minced
- Zest and juice of 1 lemon
- 2 tablespoons olive oil
- Salt and pepper, to taste
- Red pepper flakes, optional, for heat
- Fresh parsley, chopped, for garnish

Instructions:

1. Prepare the Zucchini Noodles (Zoodles):
   - Using a spiralizer or a julienne peeler, spiralize the zucchini into noodles. Alternatively, you can use a vegetable peeler to create thin, ribbon-like strips.
   - Place the zucchini noodles in a colander and sprinkle with salt. Let them sit for about 10-15 minutes to release excess moisture. Afterward, pat them dry with paper towels.
2. Cook the Shrimp:
   - In a large skillet, heat 1 tablespoon of olive oil over medium-high heat. Add minced garlic and cook for about 1 minute until fragrant.
   - Add the shrimp to the skillet in a single layer. Season with salt, pepper, and red pepper flakes (if using). Cook the shrimp for 2-3 minutes on each side until they turn pink and opaque. Remove the shrimp from the skillet and set aside.
3. Make the Lemon Garlic Sauce:
   - In the same skillet, add the remaining tablespoon of olive oil. Add lemon zest and stir for a few seconds to release the flavors.
   - Add the zucchini noodles to the skillet. Toss and sauté for 2-3 minutes until the noodles are just tender but still crisp.
   - Add lemon juice to the skillet and toss everything together. Adjust seasoning with salt and pepper if needed.
4. Combine and Serve:
   - Return the cooked shrimp to the skillet with the zucchini noodles. Toss gently to combine and heat through for another minute or so.
   - Remove from heat and garnish with chopped fresh parsley.
5. Serve:
   - Serve the Lemon Garlic Shrimp with Zucchini Noodles immediately. Enjoy this light and healthy dish as a main course.

This dish is not only delicious but also quick and easy to prepare. It's perfect for a light lunch or dinner, especially if you're looking for a low-carb option. Adjust the seasoning and spice level according to your taste preferences.

Black Bean and Corn Quesadillas

Ingredients:

- 4 large flour tortillas
- 1 can (15 oz) black beans, drained and rinsed
- 1 cup corn kernels (fresh, canned, or frozen)
- 1 cup shredded cheese (cheddar, Monterey Jack, or a blend)
- 1/2 cup diced red bell pepper
- 1/4 cup chopped fresh cilantro (optional)
- 1 teaspoon ground cumin
- 1/2 teaspoon chili powder
- Salt and pepper, to taste
- Cooking spray or vegetable oil, for cooking

Optional toppings:

- Salsa
- Guacamole or sliced avocado
- Sour cream or Greek yogurt
- Chopped fresh cilantro
- Lime wedges

Instructions:

1. Prepare the Filling:
    - In a medium bowl, combine black beans, corn kernels, diced red bell pepper, chopped cilantro (if using), ground cumin, chili powder, salt, and pepper. Mix well to combine.
2. Assemble the Quesadillas:
    - Lay out one tortilla on a clean surface. Sprinkle about 1/4 cup of shredded cheese evenly over one half of the tortilla.
    - Spoon a generous amount of the black bean and corn mixture over the cheese. Spread it out evenly.
    - Sprinkle a little more cheese on top of the filling if desired.
    - Fold the tortilla in half over the filling to create a half-moon shape.
3. Cook the Quesadillas:
    - Heat a large skillet or griddle over medium heat. Lightly coat the skillet with cooking spray or brush with a little vegetable oil.
    - Place the assembled quesadilla in the skillet and cook for about 3-4 minutes per side, or until the tortilla is golden brown and crispy, and the cheese is melted.
    - Press down gently with a spatula while cooking to help seal the quesadilla and evenly melt the cheese.
    - Remove the quesadilla from the skillet and transfer to a cutting board. Let it cool for a minute before slicing into wedges.

4. Repeat:
    - Repeat the assembling and cooking process with the remaining tortillas and filling ingredients.
5. Serve:
    - Serve the black bean and corn quesadillas hot, with optional toppings such as salsa, guacamole or avocado slices, sour cream or Greek yogurt, chopped fresh cilantro, and lime wedges on the side.

Enjoy your homemade Black Bean and Corn Quesadillas! They make a delicious and versatile meal that's perfect for a quick lunch, dinner, or even as a party appetizer.

Greek Chicken Bowls

Ingredients:

For the Chicken:

- 1 lb (450g) chicken breast, boneless and skinless
- 2 tablespoons olive oil
- Juice of 1 lemon
- 2 cloves garlic, minced
- 1 teaspoon dried oregano
- Salt and pepper, to taste

For the Tzatziki Sauce:

- 1 cup Greek yogurt
- 1/2 cucumber, grated and excess liquid squeezed out
- 1 clove garlic, minced
- 1 tablespoon fresh dill, chopped (or 1 teaspoon dried dill)
- Juice of 1/2 lemon
- Salt and pepper, to taste

For the Bowl:

- Cooked quinoa or brown rice
- Cherry tomatoes, halved
- Cucumber, diced
- Red onion, thinly sliced
- Kalamata olives, pitted and sliced
- Feta cheese, crumbled
- Fresh parsley or mint, chopped for garnish
- Optional: Hummus, pita bread or flatbread

Instructions:

1. Marinate the Chicken:
    - In a bowl or resealable plastic bag, combine olive oil, lemon juice, minced garlic, dried oregano, salt, and pepper. Add chicken breasts and coat them evenly with the marinade. Let it marinate in the refrigerator for at least 30 minutes, or up to 4 hours.
2. Make the Tzatziki Sauce:
    - In a bowl, combine Greek yogurt, grated cucumber (squeeze out excess liquid), minced garlic, chopped dill, lemon juice, salt, and pepper. Stir well to combine. Adjust seasoning to taste. Refrigerate until ready to use.
3. Grill the Chicken:

- Preheat a grill or grill pan over medium-high heat. Grill the marinated chicken breasts for about 6-7 minutes per side, or until cooked through and no longer pink in the center. Cooking time may vary depending on the thickness of the chicken breasts. Remove from heat and let the chicken rest for a few minutes before slicing.
4. Assemble the Bowls:
    - Divide cooked quinoa or brown rice among serving bowls.
    - Arrange sliced grilled chicken, cherry tomatoes, diced cucumber, thinly sliced red onion, Kalamata olives, and crumbled feta cheese on top of the quinoa or rice.
    - Drizzle tzatziki sauce over the bowls.
    - Garnish with chopped fresh parsley or mint.
5. Serve:
    - Serve the Greek Chicken Bowls immediately, optionally with hummus and pita bread or flatbread on the side.

Enjoy your homemade Greek Chicken Bowls! They are packed with fresh flavors and can be customized with your favorite Mediterranean ingredients. Adjust the toppings and quantities according to your taste preferences.

Lentil Soup

Ingredients:

- 1 cup dried lentils (green or brown), rinsed and picked over
- 1 onion, diced
- 2 carrots, diced
- 2 celery stalks, diced
- 3 cloves garlic, minced
- 1 can (14 oz) diced tomatoes
- 6 cups vegetable or chicken broth
- 1 teaspoon dried thyme
- 1 teaspoon ground cumin
- 1/2 teaspoon paprika
- Salt and pepper, to taste
- 2 tablespoons olive oil
- Optional garnishes: Fresh chopped parsley, a squeeze of lemon juice, crusty bread

Instructions:

1. Prepare Lentils:
    - Rinse the lentils under cold water and pick out any debris. Set aside.
2. Sauté Vegetables:
    - Heat olive oil in a large pot or Dutch oven over medium heat. Add diced onion, carrots, and celery. Cook, stirring occasionally, for about 5-7 minutes until the vegetables begin to soften.
3. Add Garlic and Spices:
    - Add minced garlic, dried thyme, ground cumin, and paprika to the pot. Stir and cook for 1 minute until fragrant.
4. Simmer Soup:
    - Pour in the diced tomatoes (with their juices) and the rinsed lentils. Stir to combine.
    - Add the vegetable or chicken broth to the pot. Bring the soup to a boil, then reduce the heat to low. Cover and simmer for about 30-35 minutes, or until the lentils are tender.
5. Season and Serve:
    - Season the lentil soup with salt and pepper, adjusting to taste.
    - If desired, use an immersion blender to partially blend the soup for a creamier texture, leaving some lentils whole for texture.
    - Serve hot, garnished with fresh chopped parsley and a squeeze of lemon juice if desired. Enjoy with crusty bread on the side.

This lentil soup is versatile and can be adapted based on your preferences. You can add more vegetables like spinach or kale, or adjust the spices to suit your taste. It's perfect for a comforting meal on a cold day and leftovers can be stored in the refrigerator for a few days or frozen for longer storage.

BBQ Pulled Pork Sandwiches

Ingredients:

For the Pulled Pork:

- 3-4 lbs (about 1.5-2 kg) pork shoulder or pork butt, boneless
- 1 onion, sliced
- 4 cloves garlic, minced
- 1 cup chicken broth or water
- 1 cup BBQ sauce (plus extra for serving)
- 2 tablespoons brown sugar
- 1 tablespoon smoked paprika
- 1 tablespoon Worcestershire sauce
- 1 teaspoon ground cumin
- Salt and pepper, to taste

For Serving:

- Hamburger buns or sandwich rolls
- Coleslaw (optional, for topping)

Instructions:

1. Prepare the Pork:
    - Season the pork shoulder with salt and pepper on all sides.
    - In a large skillet or Dutch oven, heat a tablespoon of oil over medium-high heat. Sear the pork shoulder on all sides until browned, about 3-4 minutes per side. Remove and set aside.
2. Slow Cook the Pork:
    - In the same skillet or Dutch oven, add sliced onion and minced garlic. Sauté for 2-3 minutes until softened.
    - Return the seared pork shoulder to the skillet. Add chicken broth (or water), BBQ sauce, brown sugar, smoked paprika, Worcestershire sauce, and ground cumin. Stir to combine, making sure the pork is coated with the sauce.
3. Cook the Pork:
    - Cover the skillet or Dutch oven with a lid. Reduce the heat to low and simmer for 6-8 hours, or until the pork is very tender and easily shreds with a fork. Alternatively, you can transfer everything to a slow cooker and cook on low for 8-10 hours or high for 4-6 hours.
4. Shred the Pork:
    - Once the pork is cooked and tender, remove it from the cooking liquid and transfer to a cutting board or large plate. Use two forks to shred the pork into bite-sized pieces. Discard any large pieces of fat.
5. Finish the Sauce:

- If desired, skim off excess fat from the cooking liquid in the skillet or Dutch oven. You can also strain the liquid and reduce it in a separate saucepan over medium heat until thickened, then mix it back with the shredded pork for a more concentrated flavor.

6. Assemble the Sandwiches:
    - Toast the hamburger buns or sandwich rolls lightly, if desired.
    - Pile the shredded BBQ pulled pork onto the bottom half of each bun.
    - Drizzle additional BBQ sauce over the pork if desired.
    - Top with coleslaw for added crunch and freshness, if desired.
    - Place the top half of the bun over the pork and serve immediately.

Enjoy your homemade BBQ Pulled Pork Sandwiches! They're perfect for gatherings, game day, or a satisfying family meal. Adjust the seasoning and sauce according to your taste preference for a personalized touch.

Caprese Pasta Salad

Ingredients:

- 8 oz (225g) pasta (such as penne, fusilli, or rotini)
- 1 pint cherry tomatoes, halved
- 1 ball fresh mozzarella cheese, diced or pearls
- 1/4 cup fresh basil leaves, thinly sliced or torn
- 2 tablespoons extra virgin olive oil
- 1 tablespoon balsamic vinegar (or balsamic glaze)
- Salt and freshly ground black pepper, to taste

Optional Additions:

- 1/4 cup pitted Kalamata olives, sliced
- 1/4 cup sliced red onion
- Freshly grated Parmesan cheese, for garnish

Instructions:

1. Cook the Pasta:
    - Bring a large pot of salted water to a boil. Cook the pasta according to package instructions until al dente. Drain and rinse under cold water to stop the cooking process. Drain well again.
2. Prepare the Salad:
    - In a large bowl, combine the cooked and cooled pasta with cherry tomatoes, diced mozzarella (or mozzarella pearls), and sliced basil leaves.
    - If using, add sliced Kalamata olives and sliced red onion.
3. Dress the Salad:
    - Drizzle extra virgin olive oil and balsamic vinegar (or balsamic glaze) over the salad ingredients.
    - Season with salt and freshly ground black pepper, to taste. Toss gently to combine and coat everything evenly with the dressing.
4. Chill and Serve:
    - Cover the bowl with plastic wrap or transfer the salad to an airtight container. Refrigerate for at least 30 minutes to allow the flavors to meld together.
5. Garnish and Serve:
    - Before serving, give the Caprese Pasta Salad a final toss. Taste and adjust seasoning if needed.
    - Optionally, garnish with freshly grated Parmesan cheese and additional basil leaves.
6. Serve:
    - Serve the Caprese Pasta Salad chilled or at room temperature as a side dish or light main course. It's perfect for picnics, potlucks, or as a refreshing summer meal.

Enjoy your homemade Caprese Pasta Salad! It's versatile, easy to customize with additional ingredients, and showcases the vibrant flavors of fresh tomatoes, mozzarella, and basil.

Cauliflower Fried Rice

Ingredients:

- 1 medium head of cauliflower, cut into florets
- 2 tablespoons sesame oil or olive oil
- 2 cloves garlic, minced
- 1 small onion, diced
- 1 cup mixed vegetables (such as peas, carrots, and corn)
- 2 eggs, lightly beaten
- 3 tablespoons soy sauce (or tamari for gluten-free)
- 1 tablespoon oyster sauce (optional)
- 1 teaspoon grated ginger (optional)
- Salt and pepper, to taste
- Green onions, chopped, for garnish
- Sesame seeds, for garnish

Instructions:

1. Prepare the Cauliflower Rice:
    - Place cauliflower florets in a food processor. Pulse several times until cauliflower resembles rice grains. Alternatively, you can grate the cauliflower using a box grater.
2. Cook the Cauliflower Rice:
    - Heat 1 tablespoon of sesame oil or olive oil in a large skillet or wok over medium heat. Add minced garlic and diced onion. Cook for 2-3 minutes until onion becomes translucent.
    - Add the cauliflower rice to the skillet. Stir-fry for 4-5 minutes, stirring occasionally, until the cauliflower is tender but still has a slight crunch. Season with salt and pepper to taste. Remove cauliflower rice from the skillet and set aside.
3. Cook the Vegetables and Eggs:
    - In the same skillet, heat the remaining tablespoon of oil over medium heat. Add mixed vegetables (peas, carrots, corn) and stir-fry for 3-4 minutes until vegetables are heated through.
    - Push the vegetables to one side of the skillet. Pour beaten eggs into the empty side of the skillet. Scramble the eggs until cooked through, breaking them into small pieces with a spatula.
4. Combine Everything:
    - Return the cooked cauliflower rice to the skillet with the vegetables and eggs. Stir everything together to combine.
5. Season the Fried Rice:
    - Drizzle soy sauce (or tamari) and oyster sauce (if using) over the cauliflower fried rice. Add grated ginger for extra flavor if desired. Stir well to coat everything evenly. Taste and adjust seasoning with salt and pepper if needed.
6. Serve:

- Remove from heat and garnish with chopped green onions and sesame seeds.
- Serve the cauliflower fried rice hot as a main dish or side dish. Enjoy!

Cauliflower fried rice is low-carb, gluten-free, and packed with vegetables, making it a healthy alternative to traditional fried rice. Customize the recipe by adding protein like cooked chicken, shrimp, or tofu if desired.

Moroccan Couscous with Chickpeas

Ingredients:

- 1 cup couscous
- 1 tablespoon olive oil
- 1 onion, finely chopped
- 2 cloves garlic, minced
- 1 teaspoon ground cumin
- 1 teaspoon ground coriander
- 1/2 teaspoon ground cinnamon
- 1/2 teaspoon ground turmeric
- 1/4 teaspoon ground ginger
- Pinch of saffron threads (optional)
- 1 can (15 oz) chickpeas, drained and rinsed
- 1 cup vegetable broth or water
- 1 cup diced tomatoes (canned or fresh)
- 1/2 cup chopped dried apricots or raisins
- Zest and juice of 1 lemon
- Salt and pepper, to taste
- Fresh cilantro or parsley, chopped, for garnish

Instructions:

1. Prepare the Couscous:
    - Place couscous in a bowl and cover with boiling water or vegetable broth. Cover the bowl with a lid or plate and let it sit for about 5-10 minutes until the couscous absorbs the liquid and becomes fluffy. Fluff with a fork to separate the grains.
2. Cook the Spices and Aromatics:
    - Heat olive oil in a large skillet or pot over medium heat. Add chopped onion and sauté for 3-4 minutes until softened.
    - Add minced garlic, ground cumin, ground coriander, ground cinnamon, ground turmeric, ground ginger, and saffron threads (if using). Stir and cook for 1 minute until fragrant.
3. Add Chickpeas and Tomatoes:
    - Add drained and rinsed chickpeas to the skillet. Stir to combine with the spices and onions.
    - Pour in vegetable broth (or water) and diced tomatoes. Bring to a simmer and cook for about 5-7 minutes until the sauce slightly thickens and flavors meld together.
4. Combine with Couscous:
    - Add cooked couscous to the skillet with the chickpea mixture. Stir gently to combine, ensuring the couscous is well coated with the sauce.

- Stir in chopped dried apricots (or raisins), lemon zest, and lemon juice. Season with salt and pepper to taste. Adjust seasoning and sweetness with more lemon juice or dried fruit if desired.
5. Serve:
    - Remove from heat and transfer Moroccan couscous with chickpeas to serving plates or bowls.
    - Garnish with chopped fresh cilantro or parsley.
    - Serve warm as a main dish or side dish. Enjoy the delicious flavors of Moroccan-inspired couscous!

This Moroccan couscous with chickpeas dish is hearty, aromatic, and packed with warm spices and sweet dried fruit, making it a perfect meal for lunch or dinner. Adjust the spice levels according to your preference and serve with a side of yogurt or a green salad if desired.

Teriyaki Chicken Lettuce Wraps

Ingredients:

- 1 lb (450g) boneless, skinless chicken breasts or thighs, cut into small pieces
- 1/2 cup teriyaki sauce (store-bought or homemade)
- 2 tablespoons soy sauce (or tamari for gluten-free option)
- 1 tablespoon honey or brown sugar
- 2 cloves garlic, minced
- 1 teaspoon grated ginger
- 1 tablespoon sesame oil
- 1 tablespoon vegetable oil
- 1 head of iceberg or butter lettuce, leaves separated
- 1 cup cooked rice (optional, for serving)
- Thinly sliced green onions, for garnish
- Sesame seeds, for garnish

Instructions:

1. Marinate the Chicken:
    - In a bowl, combine teriyaki sauce, soy sauce, honey (or brown sugar), minced garlic, and grated ginger. Stir until well combined.
    - Add the chicken pieces to the marinade and toss to coat evenly. Let it marinate for at least 15-20 minutes in the refrigerator.
2. Cook the Chicken:
    - Heat sesame oil and vegetable oil in a large skillet or wok over medium-high heat.
    - Add the marinated chicken pieces (reserving the marinade) to the skillet in a single layer. Cook for about 5-7 minutes, stirring occasionally, until the chicken is cooked through and caramelized. Ensure the internal temperature reaches 165°F (74°C).
    - Pour in the reserved marinade and cook for an additional 2-3 minutes until the sauce thickens and coats the chicken. Remove from heat.
3. Assemble the Lettuce Wraps:
    - Arrange the lettuce leaves on a serving platter.
    - Spoon a small amount of cooked rice (if using) onto each lettuce leaf, if desired.
    - Spoon the teriyaki chicken mixture into each lettuce leaf.
    - Garnish with thinly sliced green onions and sesame seeds.
4. Serve:
    - Serve the teriyaki chicken lettuce wraps immediately while warm.
    - Optionally, serve with additional teriyaki sauce on the side for dipping.

Enjoy your homemade Teriyaki Chicken Lettuce Wraps! They are light, flavorful, and can be customized with your favorite toppings or additional vegetables like shredded carrots, cucumber, or bell peppers.

Spinach and Feta Stuffed Chicken Breast

Ingredients:

- 4 boneless, skinless chicken breasts
- Salt and pepper, to taste
- 1 tablespoon olive oil

For the Spinach and Feta Stuffing:

- 2 cups fresh spinach, chopped
- 1/2 cup crumbled feta cheese
- 1/4 cup grated Parmesan cheese
- 2 cloves garlic, minced
- 1 tablespoon olive oil
- Salt and pepper, to taste
- Pinch of nutmeg (optional)

Instructions:

1. Prepare the Spinach and Feta Stuffing:
    - Heat 1 tablespoon of olive oil in a skillet over medium heat. Add minced garlic and cook for about 30 seconds until fragrant.
    - Add chopped spinach to the skillet and cook until wilted, about 2-3 minutes.
    - Remove from heat and transfer the cooked spinach to a mixing bowl. Let it cool slightly.
    - To the bowl with spinach, add crumbled feta cheese, grated Parmesan cheese, salt, pepper, and a pinch of nutmeg (if using). Mix well to combine.
2. Prepare the Chicken Breasts:
    - Preheat the oven to 375°F (190°C).
    - Use a sharp knife to make a horizontal slit along the side of each chicken breast to create a pocket. Be careful not to cut all the way through.
    - Season the chicken breasts with salt and pepper, both inside and out.
3. Stuff the Chicken Breasts:
    - Stuff each chicken breast with the spinach and feta mixture, dividing it evenly among the breasts. Use toothpicks to secure the openings if necessary.
4. Cook the Chicken:
    - Heat 1 tablespoon of olive oil in an oven-safe skillet over medium-high heat.
    - Carefully place stuffed chicken breasts in the skillet and sear for 3-4 minutes on each side until golden brown.
5. Finish in the Oven:
    - Transfer the skillet to the preheated oven and bake for 20-25 minutes, or until the chicken is cooked through and reaches an internal temperature of 165°F (74°C).
6. Serve:
    - Remove the spinach and feta stuffed chicken breasts from the oven.

- Let them rest for a few minutes before serving.
- Optionally, garnish with chopped fresh herbs like parsley or basil before serving.

7. **Serve:**
    - Serve the spinach and feta stuffed chicken breasts hot, alongside your favorite side dishes like roasted vegetables, mashed potatoes, or a fresh green salad.

Enjoy your flavorful Spinach and Feta Stuffed Chicken Breast! It's a dish that combines juicy chicken with creamy feta and spinach for a delightful meal.

Spaghetti Squash Pad Thai

Ingredients:

- 1 medium spaghetti squash
- 2 tablespoons vegetable oil (divided)
- 2 cloves garlic, minced
- 1 small onion, thinly sliced
- 1 red bell pepper, thinly sliced
- 1 cup shredded carrots
- 1 cup bean sprouts
- 2 green onions, chopped (green and white parts separated)
- 1/4 cup chopped peanuts, for garnish
- Lime wedges, for serving
- Fresh cilantro, for garnish

For the Sauce:

- 3 tablespoons soy sauce (or tamari for gluten-free)
- 2 tablespoons fish sauce (omit for vegetarian/vegan option)
- 1 tablespoon rice vinegar
- 1 tablespoon brown sugar (or coconut sugar)
- 1 tablespoon Sriracha sauce (adjust to taste)
- Juice of 1 lime

Instructions:

1. Prepare the Spaghetti Squash:
    - Preheat your oven to 400°F (200°C).
    - Cut the spaghetti squash in half lengthwise and scoop out the seeds.
    - Drizzle the cut sides with 1 tablespoon of vegetable oil and season with salt and pepper.
    - Place the squash halves cut side down on a baking sheet lined with parchment paper.
    - Roast in the oven for 30-40 minutes, or until the squash is tender and easily pierced with a fork.
    - Remove from the oven and let it cool slightly. Use a fork to scrape the flesh of the squash into spaghetti-like strands. Set aside.
2. Make the Sauce:
    - In a small bowl, whisk together soy sauce, fish sauce (if using), rice vinegar, brown sugar, Sriracha sauce, and lime juice. Set aside.
3. Cook the Vegetables:
    - Heat the remaining 1 tablespoon of vegetable oil in a large skillet or wok over medium-high heat.

- Add minced garlic and white parts of the chopped green onions. Cook for 1 minute until fragrant.
- Add sliced onion and red bell pepper. Stir-fry for 2-3 minutes until vegetables begin to soften.

4. Assemble the Pad Thai:
    - Add shredded carrots and bean sprouts to the skillet. Cook for another 2 minutes, stirring frequently.
    - Add the spaghetti squash strands to the skillet along with the prepared sauce. Toss everything together until well combined and heated through, about 2-3 minutes.
5. Serve:
    - Divide the spaghetti squash Pad Thai among serving plates or bowls.
    - Garnish with chopped peanuts, chopped cilantro, and the remaining green parts of the chopped green onions.
    - Serve with lime wedges on the side for squeezing over the dish.

Enjoy your Spaghetti Squash Pad Thai as a nutritious and flavorful alternative to the classic dish! It's packed with vegetables and the sauce brings the authentic Thai flavors to life.

Chili con Carne

Ingredients:

- 1 lb (450g) ground beef (or ground turkey)
- 1 onion, diced
- 3 cloves garlic, minced
- 1 bell pepper, diced (any color)
- 1 can (15 oz) kidney beans, drained and rinsed
- 1 can (15 oz) black beans, drained and rinsed
- 1 can (15 oz) diced tomatoes
- 1 can (6 oz) tomato paste
- 2 cups beef broth (or chicken broth)
- 2 tablespoons chili powder
- 1 teaspoon ground cumin
- 1 teaspoon paprika
- 1/2 teaspoon dried oregano
- 1/2 teaspoon cayenne pepper (adjust to taste, for spiciness)
- Salt and pepper, to taste
- 1 tablespoon olive oil
- Optional toppings: Shredded cheese, sour cream, sliced green onions, chopped cilantro, avocado slices

Instructions:

1. Brown the Meat:
    - Heat olive oil in a large pot or Dutch oven over medium-high heat. Add ground beef and cook until browned, breaking it up with a spoon as it cooks.
2. Add Aromatics:
    - Add diced onion, minced garlic, and diced bell pepper to the pot. Cook for 3-4 minutes until vegetables are softened and fragrant.
3. Add Beans and Tomatoes:
    - Stir in kidney beans, black beans, diced tomatoes, and tomato paste. Mix well to combine.
4. Season the Chili:
    - Add chili powder, ground cumin, paprika, dried oregano, cayenne pepper, salt, and pepper to the pot. Stir to evenly distribute the spices.
5. Simmer:
    - Pour in beef broth (or chicken broth) and bring the mixture to a simmer. Reduce heat to low, cover, and let it simmer for at least 30 minutes to allow the flavors to meld together. Stir occasionally.
6. Adjust Seasoning:
    - Taste the chili and adjust seasoning as needed. Add more salt, pepper, or chili powder for more heat, if desired.
7. Serve:

- Ladle the chili into bowls and serve hot.
- Garnish with shredded cheese, sour cream, sliced green onions, chopped cilantro, or avocado slices, if desired.

Enjoy your homemade Chili con Carne! It's a comforting and satisfying dish that's perfect for cooler days or any time you're craving a hearty meal.

Sweet Potato and Black Bean Tacos

Ingredients:

- 2 medium sweet potatoes, peeled and diced into small cubes
- 1 can (15 oz) black beans, drained and rinsed
- 1 tablespoon olive oil
- 1 teaspoon ground cumin
- 1 teaspoon chili powder
- 1/2 teaspoon paprika
- Salt and pepper, to taste
- 8 small corn or flour tortillas
- Optional toppings: Salsa, avocado slices or guacamole, shredded lettuce or cabbage, diced tomatoes, sour cream or Greek yogurt, chopped cilantro, lime wedges

Instructions:

1. Roast the Sweet Potatoes:
    - Preheat your oven to 400°F (200°C).
    - Toss diced sweet potatoes with olive oil, ground cumin, chili powder, paprika, salt, and pepper in a large bowl until evenly coated.
    - Spread the sweet potatoes in a single layer on a baking sheet lined with parchment paper.
    - Roast in the preheated oven for 20-25 minutes, stirring halfway through, until sweet potatoes are tender and lightly browned.
2. Prepare the Black Beans:
    - While the sweet potatoes are roasting, heat a small skillet over medium heat.
    - Add drained and rinsed black beans to the skillet. Stir in a pinch of cumin, chili powder, paprika, salt, and pepper to taste. Cook for 5-7 minutes, stirring occasionally, until heated through.
3. Warm the Tortillas:
    - In the last few minutes of cooking, wrap tortillas in foil and warm them in the oven alongside the sweet potatoes until heated through.
4. Assemble the Tacos:
    - Fill each warmed tortilla with roasted sweet potatoes and black beans.
    - Add your choice of toppings such as salsa, avocado slices or guacamole, shredded lettuce or cabbage, diced tomatoes, sour cream or Greek yogurt, chopped cilantro, and a squeeze of lime juice.
5. Serve:
    - Serve the sweet potato and black bean tacos immediately.
    - Enjoy the delicious flavors and textures of these vegetarian tacos!

These Sweet Potato and Black Bean Tacos are not only tasty but also nutritious and versatile. Feel free to customize them with your favorite toppings or add a drizzle of hot sauce for extra kick. They make a perfect meal for Meatless Mondays or any day of the week!

Pesto Pasta with Cherry Tomatoes

Ingredients:

- 8 oz (225g) pasta of your choice (such as spaghetti, penne, or fusilli)
- 1 cup cherry tomatoes, halved
- 1/2 cup basil pesto (store-bought or homemade)
- 1/4 cup grated Parmesan cheese
- Salt and pepper, to taste
- Fresh basil leaves, chopped, for garnish (optional)

Instructions:

1. Cook the Pasta:
    - Bring a large pot of salted water to a boil. Cook the pasta according to package instructions until al dente. Reserve about 1/2 cup of pasta cooking water before draining.
2. Prepare the Cherry Tomatoes:
    - While the pasta is cooking, halve the cherry tomatoes and set them aside.
3. Combine Pasta and Pesto:
    - In a large skillet or saucepan, add the cooked pasta and cherry tomatoes.
    - Stir in the basil pesto until the pasta and tomatoes are evenly coated. If the pesto sauce seems too thick, add some of the reserved pasta cooking water a little at a time to loosen it up.
4. Season and Garnish:
    - Add grated Parmesan cheese to the pasta and stir until well combined.
    - Season with salt and pepper to taste. Remember, pesto and Parmesan are already salty, so adjust accordingly.
5. Serve:
    - Divide the pesto pasta with cherry tomatoes among serving plates or bowls.
    - Garnish with chopped fresh basil leaves if desired.
    - Serve immediately and enjoy the vibrant flavors of this simple and delicious dish!

Pesto Pasta with Cherry Tomatoes is a quick and flavorful meal that's perfect for a weeknight dinner or a casual gathering. You can also add grilled chicken, shrimp, or roasted vegetables to make it even heartier. It's versatile and sure to be a crowd-pleaser!

Eggplant Parmesan

Ingredients:

- 2 medium eggplants, sliced into 1/2-inch rounds
- Salt, for sweating the eggplant
- 1 cup all-purpose flour
- 2-3 eggs, beaten
- 2 cups breadcrumbs (plain or seasoned)
- 1 cup grated Parmesan cheese
- 2 cups marinara sauce (store-bought or homemade)
- 2 cups shredded mozzarella cheese
- Fresh basil leaves, chopped, for garnish (optional)

Instructions:

1. Prepare the Eggplant:
    - Place the eggplant slices in a colander and sprinkle each layer generously with salt. Let them sit for about 30 minutes to release excess moisture. This helps to reduce bitterness in the eggplant.
2. Breading the Eggplant:
    - Preheat the oven to 400°F (200°C). Line a baking sheet with parchment paper.
    - Pat the eggplant slices dry with paper towels to remove excess moisture.
    - Set up a breading station: Place flour in one shallow bowl, beaten eggs in another bowl, and breadcrumbs mixed with grated Parmesan cheese in a third bowl.
    - Dredge each eggplant slice first in the flour, shaking off any excess, then dip into the beaten eggs, and finally coat evenly with the breadcrumb mixture. Press lightly to adhere the breadcrumbs.
3. Bake the Eggplant:
    - Place the breaded eggplant slices on the prepared baking sheet in a single layer.
    - Bake in the preheated oven for 20-25 minutes, flipping halfway through, until the eggplant is golden and crispy. Remove from the oven and reduce the oven temperature to 350°F (175°C).
4. Assemble the Eggplant Parmesan:
    - Spread a thin layer of marinara sauce on the bottom of a baking dish.
    - Arrange a layer of baked eggplant slices on top of the sauce.
    - Spoon marinara sauce over each eggplant slice, followed by a sprinkle of shredded mozzarella cheese.
    - Repeat layers, ending with a layer of marinara sauce and shredded mozzarella cheese on top.
5. Bake:
    - Cover the baking dish with foil and bake in the 350°F (175°C) oven for 20-25 minutes, until the cheese is melted and bubbly.
6. Serve:

- - Remove from the oven and let it cool slightly before serving.
  - Garnish with chopped fresh basil leaves if desired.
  - Serve Eggplant Parmesan hot as a main dish, accompanied by a side of pasta or a green salad.

Enjoy your homemade Eggplant Parmesan! It's a comforting and flavorful dish that's perfect for vegetarians or anyone looking to enjoy a delicious Italian-inspired meal.

Lemon Herb Grilled Chicken

Ingredients:

- 4 boneless, skinless chicken breasts
- Zest and juice of 1 lemon
- 2 cloves garlic, minced
- 2 tablespoons fresh herbs (such as rosemary, thyme, and/or oregano), chopped
- 2 tablespoons olive oil
- Salt and pepper, to taste

Instructions:

1. Prepare the Marinade:
    - In a small bowl, whisk together lemon zest, lemon juice, minced garlic, chopped fresh herbs, olive oil, salt, and pepper.
2. Marinate the Chicken:
    - Place chicken breasts in a shallow dish or resealable plastic bag.
    - Pour the marinade over the chicken, making sure it's evenly coated. Marinate in the refrigerator for at least 30 minutes, or up to 4 hours for maximum flavor.
3. Preheat the Grill:
    - Preheat your grill to medium-high heat (about 400°F to 450°F).
4. Grill the Chicken:
    - Remove chicken breasts from the marinade and discard the marinade.
    - Grill the chicken for 6-7 minutes per side, or until the internal temperature reaches 165°F (74°C) and the chicken is no longer pink in the center.
    - Cooking times may vary depending on the thickness of the chicken breasts. Use a meat thermometer to ensure they are fully cooked.
5. Rest and Serve:
    - Remove the grilled chicken from the grill and let it rest for a few minutes before slicing or serving whole.
    - Garnish with additional fresh herbs and lemon slices if desired.
6. Serve:
    - Serve the Lemon Herb Grilled Chicken hot, accompanied by your favorite side dishes such as grilled vegetables, salad, or rice.

Enjoy your flavorful and tender Lemon Herb Grilled Chicken! It's a simple yet elegant dish that's sure to impress with its bright citrus and herb flavors.

Mexican Quinoa Stuffed Peppers

Ingredients:

- 4 large bell peppers (any color), tops cut off and seeds removed
- 1 cup quinoa, rinsed
- 1 can (15 oz) black beans, drained and rinsed
- 1 cup corn kernels (fresh, canned, or frozen)
- 1 can (14.5 oz) diced tomatoes, drained
- 1 teaspoon chili powder
- 1 teaspoon ground cumin
- 1/2 teaspoon paprika
- Salt and pepper, to taste
- 1 cup shredded cheese (cheddar, Monterey Jack, or Mexican blend)
- Optional toppings: Chopped fresh cilantro, avocado slices, sour cream, salsa

Instructions:

1. Prepare the Quinoa:
    - In a medium saucepan, combine quinoa and 2 cups of water. Bring to a boil over medium-high heat.
    - Reduce heat to low, cover, and simmer for 15-20 minutes, or until quinoa is cooked and water is absorbed. Remove from heat and let it sit covered for 5 minutes. Fluff with a fork.
2. Prepare the Stuffed Peppers:
    - Preheat your oven to 375°F (190°C).
    - In a large bowl, combine cooked quinoa, black beans, corn kernels, diced tomatoes, chili powder, cumin, paprika, salt, and pepper. Mix well to combine.
3. Stuff the Peppers:
    - Place the hollowed-out bell peppers upright in a baking dish.
    - Spoon the quinoa and bean mixture evenly into each bell pepper until they are filled to the top.
    - Sprinkle shredded cheese over the top of each stuffed pepper.
4. Bake:
    - Cover the baking dish with foil and bake in the preheated oven for 30-35 minutes, or until the peppers are tender and the filling is heated through.
    - If you prefer a more roasted appearance on the peppers, you can remove the foil during the last 10 minutes of baking.
5. Serve:
    - Remove from the oven and let the stuffed peppers cool slightly before serving.
    - Garnish with chopped fresh cilantro, avocado slices, sour cream, or salsa, if desired.

Enjoy your delicious and nutritious Mexican Quinoa Stuffed Peppers! They make a satisfying vegetarian main dish or a flavorful side dish for any occasion.

Tuna Salad Lettuce Wraps

Ingredients:

- 2 cans (5 oz each) tuna, drained
- 1/4 cup mayonnaise (or Greek yogurt for a lighter option)
- 1 tablespoon Dijon mustard
- 1 celery stalk, finely chopped
- 1/4 cup red onion, finely chopped
- 1 tablespoon fresh dill, chopped (or 1 teaspoon dried dill)
- Juice of 1/2 lemon
- Salt and pepper, to taste
- Lettuce leaves (such as butter lettuce, romaine, or iceberg)

Instructions:

1. Prepare the Tuna Salad:
    - In a medium bowl, combine drained tuna, mayonnaise (or Greek yogurt), Dijon mustard, chopped celery, chopped red onion, chopped fresh dill, and lemon juice.
    - Mix well until all ingredients are evenly combined. Season with salt and pepper to taste.
2. Assemble the Lettuce Wraps:
    - Arrange lettuce leaves on a serving platter or individual plates.
    - Spoon a generous amount of tuna salad mixture onto each lettuce leaf.
3. Serve:
    - Serve the tuna salad lettuce wraps immediately, and enjoy the fresh and satisfying flavors!

Optional Additions and Variations:

- Add Crunch: Mix in chopped pickles or bell peppers for extra crunch.
- Add Sweetness: Add a touch of honey or a handful of dried cranberries for a sweet contrast.
- Spice it up: Include a dash of hot sauce or sriracha for a spicy kick.

Ratatouille

Ingredients:

- 1 eggplant, diced into 1-inch cubes
- 2 zucchini, sliced
- 1 yellow bell pepper, diced
- 1 red bell pepper, diced
- 1 onion, diced
- 3 cloves garlic, minced
- 2 cups tomatoes, diced (fresh or canned)
- 2 tablespoons tomato paste
- 2 tablespoons olive oil
- 1 teaspoon dried thyme
- 1 teaspoon dried oregano
- Salt and pepper, to taste
- Fresh basil or parsley, chopped, for garnish

Instructions:

1. Prepare the Vegetables:
    - Heat 1 tablespoon of olive oil in a large skillet or Dutch oven over medium heat.
    - Add diced eggplant and cook for 5-7 minutes, until lightly browned and softened. Remove from the skillet and set aside.
    - Add another tablespoon of olive oil to the skillet. Add the onion, bell peppers, and zucchini. Cook for 5-7 minutes, until softened.

Hawaiian Chicken Skewers

Ingredients:

- 1.5 lbs (about 700g) chicken breast, cut into 1-inch cubes
- 1 red bell pepper, cut into 1-inch pieces
- 1 green bell pepper, cut into 1-inch pieces
- 1 red onion, cut into 1-inch pieces
- 1 cup pineapple chunks (fresh or canned)
- Wooden or metal skewers (if using wooden skewers, soak them in water for 30 minutes before using)

For the Marinade:

- 1/4 cup soy sauce
- 1/4 cup pineapple juice (from canned pineapple)
- 2 tablespoons brown sugar
- 2 cloves garlic, minced
- 1 tablespoon grated fresh ginger
- 1 tablespoon olive oil

For the Glaze:

- Reserved marinade
- 2 tablespoons honey
- 1 tablespoon ketchup

Instructions:

1. Prepare the Marinade:
    - In a bowl, whisk together soy sauce, pineapple juice, brown sugar, minced garlic, grated ginger, and olive oil until well combined.
2. Marinate the Chicken:
    - Place the chicken cubes in a shallow dish or resealable plastic bag.
    - Pour half of the marinade over the chicken, reserving the other half for later. Toss the chicken to coat evenly.
    - Cover or seal the dish/bag and refrigerate for at least 30 minutes, or up to 2 hours, to marinate.
3. Prepare the Glaze:
    - In a small saucepan, combine the reserved marinade, honey, and ketchup.
    - Bring to a simmer over medium heat. Cook for 5-7 minutes, stirring occasionally, until the glaze thickens slightly. Remove from heat.
4. Assemble the Skewers:
    - Preheat your grill or grill pan over medium-high heat.
    - Thread marinated chicken cubes, bell peppers, red onion, and pineapple chunks alternately onto the skewers.

5. Grill the Skewers:
    - Place the skewers on the preheated grill. Cook for 10-12 minutes, turning occasionally, until the chicken is cooked through and has nice grill marks.
6. Glaze the Skewers:
    - Brush the cooked skewers with the prepared glaze, turning them to coat evenly. Let them cook for another minute on the grill to caramelize the glaze.
7. Serve:
    - Remove the Hawaiian Chicken Skewers from the grill and transfer them to a serving platter.
    - Garnish with chopped fresh cilantro or parsley, if desired.
    - Serve hot with rice or a salad on the side.

Enjoy your delicious Hawaiian Chicken Skewers, infused with tropical flavors and perfect for a summer barbecue or any occasion!

Butternut Squash Soup

Ingredients:

- 1 medium butternut squash (about 2 lbs), peeled, seeded, and cut into 1-inch cubes
- 1 tablespoon olive oil
- 1 onion, chopped
- 2 cloves garlic, minced
- 1 carrot, peeled and chopped
- 1 celery stalk, chopped
- 4 cups vegetable broth (or chicken broth)
- 1 teaspoon dried thyme
- 1/2 teaspoon ground cinnamon
- 1/4 teaspoon ground nutmeg
- Salt and pepper, to taste
- 1/2 cup heavy cream (optional, for a creamy soup)
- Chopped fresh parsley or chives, for garnish

Instructions:

1. Roast the Butternut Squash (Optional Step):
    - Preheat your oven to 400°F (200°C).
    - Toss the cubed butternut squash with olive oil and spread it out on a baking sheet lined with parchment paper.
    - Roast in the preheated oven for 30-35 minutes, or until the squash is tender and lightly caramelized. This step enhances the flavor of the squash, but you can skip it if you prefer.
2. Cook the Vegetables:
    - In a large pot or Dutch oven, heat olive oil over medium heat.
    - Add chopped onion, garlic, carrot, and celery. Cook, stirring occasionally, for about 5-7 minutes until the vegetables are softened.
3. Simmer the Soup:
    - Add the roasted butternut squash cubes (or raw squash cubes if you skipped roasting), vegetable broth, dried thyme, ground cinnamon, and ground nutmeg to the pot.
    - Bring the mixture to a boil, then reduce the heat to low. Cover and simmer for 20-25 minutes, or until the squash and vegetables are very tender.
4. Blend the Soup:
    - Use an immersion blender directly in the pot to puree the soup until smooth and creamy. Alternatively, carefully transfer the soup in batches to a blender and blend until smooth. Be cautious with hot liquids.
5. Finish the Soup:
    - If using heavy cream, stir it into the blended soup until well combined. This step adds richness and creaminess to the soup.
    - Season with salt and pepper to taste.

6. Serve:
    - Ladle the butternut squash soup into bowls.
    - Garnish with chopped fresh parsley or chives.
    - Serve hot, optionally with a drizzle of cream or a sprinkle of extra cinnamon on top.

Enjoy your homemade Butternut Squash Soup, a comforting and nutritious dish that's perfect for any time of year!

Turkey Chili

Ingredients:

- 1 tablespoon olive oil
- 1 onion, chopped
- 3 cloves garlic, minced
- 1 bell pepper, chopped (any color)
- 1 jalapeño, seeded and finely chopped (optional, for heat)
- 1 lb (450g) ground turkey
- 2 tablespoons chili powder
- 1 teaspoon ground cumin
- 1 teaspoon dried oregano
- 1/2 teaspoon paprika
- 1/4 teaspoon cayenne pepper (adjust to taste)
- Salt and pepper, to taste
- 1 can (15 oz) kidney beans, drained and rinsed
- 1 can (15 oz) black beans, drained and rinsed
- 1 can (14.5 oz) diced tomatoes
- 1 cup chicken broth or water
- 1 tablespoon tomato paste
- Optional toppings: Shredded cheese, sour cream, chopped green onions, cilantro, avocado slices

Instructions:

1. Sauté the Vegetables:
    - Heat olive oil in a large pot or Dutch oven over medium-high heat.
    - Add chopped onion, garlic, bell pepper, and jalapeño (if using). Sauté for 5-7 minutes, until vegetables are softened.
2. Cook the Turkey:
    - Add ground turkey to the pot. Cook, breaking it up with a spoon, until turkey is browned and cooked through.
3. Season the Chili:
    - Stir in chili powder, ground cumin, dried oregano, paprika, cayenne pepper, salt, and pepper. Cook for 1-2 minutes until fragrant.
4. Add Beans, Tomatoes, and Liquid:
    - Add kidney beans, black beans, diced tomatoes (with their juices), chicken broth (or water), and tomato paste to the pot. Stir well to combine.
5. Simmer:
    - Bring the chili to a boil, then reduce the heat to low. Cover and simmer for 30-40 minutes, stirring occasionally, to allow the flavors to meld together and the chili to thicken.
6. Adjust Seasoning:

- Taste the chili and adjust seasoning with more salt, pepper, or chili powder as needed.
7. Serve:
    - Ladle the turkey chili into bowls.
    - Garnish with shredded cheese, a dollop of sour cream, chopped green onions, cilantro, or avocado slices, if desired.

Enjoy your homemade turkey chili with your favorite toppings and sides like cornbread or tortilla chips. It's a comforting and satisfying meal that's perfect for chilly evenings!

Caprese Stuffed Portobello Mushrooms

Ingredients:

- 4 large portobello mushrooms, stems removed
- 1 tablespoon olive oil
- 2 cloves garlic, minced
- Salt and pepper, to taste
- 1 cup cherry tomatoes, halved
- 1 cup fresh mozzarella balls (bocconcini), halved or quartered if large
- 1/4 cup fresh basil leaves, thinly sliced
- Balsamic glaze, for drizzling (optional)

Instructions:

1. Prepare the Portobello Mushrooms:
   - Preheat your oven to 400°F (200°C).
   - Remove the stems from the portobello mushrooms and gently scrape out the gills using a spoon. This helps create more room for stuffing and prevents excess moisture.
2. Marinate and Roast the Mushrooms:
   - In a small bowl, mix together olive oil, minced garlic, salt, and pepper.
   - Brush the mushroom caps all over with the olive oil mixture, including the edges.
3. Stuff the Mushrooms:
   - Place the mushrooms on a baking sheet, gill side up.
   - Divide cherry tomatoes and fresh mozzarella evenly among the mushroom caps.
   - Sprinkle fresh basil leaves over the tomatoes and mozzarella.
4. Bake:
   - Bake the stuffed mushrooms in the preheated oven for 15-20 minutes, or until the mushrooms are tender and the cheese is melted and slightly golden.
5. Serve:
   - Remove from the oven and let the stuffed mushrooms cool slightly.
   - Drizzle with balsamic glaze, if using.
   - Serve warm as an appetizer or a light main dish.

These Caprese Stuffed Portobello Mushrooms are flavorful, satisfying, and make a wonderful addition to any meal. They're perfect for vegetarians and anyone who loves the classic combination of tomatoes, mozzarella, and basil. Enjoy!

Veggie Frittata

Ingredients:

- 8 large eggs
- 1/2 cup milk or heavy cream
- Salt and pepper, to taste
- 1 tablespoon olive oil or butter
- 1 small onion, diced
- 1 bell pepper, diced
- 1 cup mushrooms, sliced
- 1 cup spinach, chopped
- 1/2 cup cherry tomatoes, halved
- 1/2 cup shredded cheese (such as cheddar, mozzarella, or feta)
- Fresh herbs, chopped (optional, for garnish)

Instructions:

1. Preheat the Oven:
    - Preheat your oven to 375°F (190°C).
2. Prepare the Vegetables:
    - In a large oven-safe skillet, heat olive oil or butter over medium heat.
    - Add diced onion and cook for 2-3 minutes until softened.
    - Add diced bell pepper and mushrooms. Cook for another 3-4 minutes until vegetables are tender.
    - Add chopped spinach and cherry tomatoes. Cook for 1-2 minutes until spinach is wilted. Season with salt and pepper to taste.
3. Whisk Eggs:
    - In a bowl, whisk together eggs and milk or heavy cream until well combined. Season with salt and pepper.
4. Assemble the Frittata:
    - Pour the egg mixture evenly over the cooked vegetables in the skillet.
    - Sprinkle shredded cheese evenly over the top.
5. Cook on Stovetop:
    - Cook on the stovetop for 3-4 minutes, allowing the edges to set.
6. Bake:
    - Transfer the skillet to the preheated oven.
    - Bake for 15-20 minutes, or until the frittata is set in the center and slightly golden on top.
7. Serve:
    - Remove from the oven and let it cool for a few minutes.
    - Sprinkle with chopped fresh herbs, if desired.
    - Slice into wedges and serve warm.

This Veggie Frittata is delicious on its own or paired with a side salad or crusty bread. It's a great way to enjoy a variety of vegetables and eggs in one satisfying dish!

Beef Kebabs with Chimichurri Sauce

Ingredients:

For the Beef Kebabs:

- 1.5 lbs (680g) beef sirloin or tenderloin, cut into 1-inch cubes
- 1 red bell pepper, cut into 1-inch pieces
- 1 green bell pepper, cut into 1-inch pieces
- 1 red onion, cut into 1-inch pieces
- Wooden or metal skewers (if using wooden skewers, soak them in water for 30 minutes before using)
- Salt and pepper, to taste
- Olive oil, for brushing

For the Chimichurri Sauce:

- 1 cup fresh parsley, finely chopped
- 1/2 cup fresh cilantro, finely chopped
- 3 cloves garlic, minced
- 1 shallot, finely chopped
- 1/4 cup red wine vinegar
- 1/2 cup olive oil
- 1/2 teaspoon red pepper flakes (adjust to taste)
- Salt and pepper, to taste

Instructions:

1. Prepare the Chimichurri Sauce:
    - In a bowl, combine finely chopped parsley, cilantro, minced garlic, chopped shallot, red wine vinegar, olive oil, red pepper flakes, salt, and pepper.
    - Mix well to combine. Taste and adjust seasoning if needed. Set aside to allow the flavors to meld.
2. Prepare the Beef Kebabs:
    - If using wooden skewers, soak them in water for at least 30 minutes to prevent burning.
    - Thread beef cubes, bell pepper pieces, and red onion pieces alternately onto skewers.
    - Season the kebabs with salt and pepper, and brush lightly with olive oil.
3. Grill the Kebabs:
    - Preheat your grill or grill pan over medium-high heat.
    - Place the beef kebabs on the grill and cook for about 3-4 minutes per side, or until the beef is cooked to your desired doneness and the vegetables are tender and lightly charred.
4. Serve:

- Remove the beef kebabs from the grill and let them rest for a few minutes.
- Serve the kebabs hot, drizzled with chimichurri sauce on top or on the side.
- Enjoy your flavorful and juicy beef kebabs with the fresh and tangy chimichurri sauce!

Beef kebabs with chimichurri sauce are perfect served with rice, grilled vegetables, or a fresh salad. They make a great dish for summer gatherings or any time you're craving delicious grilled flavors!

Buffalo Chicken Wraps

Ingredients:

- 2 boneless, skinless chicken breasts, cooked and shredded (about 2 cups)
- 1/2 cup buffalo sauce (adjust to taste)
- 1/4 cup ranch or blue cheese dressing
- 4 large flour tortillas
- 1 cup shredded lettuce
- 1/2 cup shredded carrots
- 1/2 cup diced celery
- 1/2 cup diced tomatoes
- 1/4 cup crumbled blue cheese (optional)
- Fresh cilantro or parsley, chopped (for garnish, optional)

Instructions:

1. Prepare the Buffalo Chicken:
    - Cook the chicken breasts (you can boil, bake, or grill them) until fully cooked through. Shred the chicken using two forks.
2. Mix the Buffalo Chicken:
    - In a bowl, combine the shredded chicken with buffalo sauce and ranch or blue cheese dressing. Mix well until the chicken is coated evenly with the sauce.
3. Assemble the Wraps:
    - Lay out the flour tortillas on a flat surface.
    - Divide the shredded lettuce, shredded carrots, diced celery, and diced tomatoes evenly among the tortillas, placing them in the center of each tortilla.
4. Add the Buffalo Chicken:
    - Spoon the buffalo chicken mixture evenly over the vegetables on each tortilla.
5. Optional Toppings:
    - Sprinkle crumbled blue cheese over the chicken mixture for added flavor (optional).
    - Garnish with chopped cilantro or parsley, if desired.
6. Wrap the Tortillas:
    - Fold in the sides of each tortilla, then roll it up tightly from the bottom to enclose the filling.
7. Serve:
    - Slice the wraps in half diagonally, if desired.
    - Serve immediately, and enjoy your delicious Buffalo Chicken Wraps!

These wraps are perfect for lunch, dinner, or even as a party appetizer. They're easy to customize with your favorite toppings and are sure to satisfy your craving for spicy buffalo chicken flavors!

Mediterranean Orzo Salad

Ingredients:

- 1 cup orzo pasta
- 1 cup cherry tomatoes, halved
- 1 cucumber, diced
- 1/2 red onion, finely chopped
- 1/2 cup Kalamata olives, sliced
- 1/2 cup crumbled feta cheese
- 1/4 cup chopped fresh parsley
- 1/4 cup chopped fresh basil
- Juice of 1 lemon
- 3 tablespoons extra virgin olive oil
- 1 clove garlic, minced
- Salt and pepper, to taste

Instructions:

1. Cook the Orzo:
    - Cook the orzo pasta according to package instructions until al dente. Drain and rinse under cold water to stop the cooking process. Drain well.
2. Prepare the Dressing:
    - In a small bowl, whisk together the lemon juice, extra virgin olive oil, minced garlic, salt, and pepper. Set aside.
3. Assemble the Salad:
    - In a large bowl, combine the cooked and cooled orzo pasta with cherry tomatoes, diced cucumber, finely chopped red onion, sliced Kalamata olives, crumbled feta cheese, chopped fresh parsley, and chopped fresh basil.
4. Add the Dressing:
    - Pour the prepared dressing over the salad ingredients in the bowl.
    - Gently toss everything together until well combined and evenly coated with the dressing.
5. Chill and Serve:
    - Cover the bowl with plastic wrap and refrigerate the Mediterranean Orzo Salad for at least 1 hour to allow the flavors to meld together.
6. Serve:
    - Before serving, give the salad a final toss.
    - Garnish with additional fresh herbs, if desired.
    - Serve chilled as a delicious side dish or a light main course.

This Mediterranean Orzo Salad is perfect for picnics, potlucks, or as a refreshing meal on a warm day. It's packed with vibrant flavors and textures from the fresh vegetables, salty olives, and tangy feta cheese, making it a delightful addition to any menu!

Baked Cod with Garlic Butter

Ingredients:

- 4 cod fillets (about 6 oz each), skinless
- Salt and pepper, to taste
- 4 tablespoons unsalted butter, melted
- 4 cloves garlic, minced
- 1 tablespoon fresh lemon juice
- 1 tablespoon chopped fresh parsley (optional, for garnish)
- Lemon wedges, for serving

Instructions:

1. Preheat the Oven:
    - Preheat your oven to 400°F (200°C).
2. Prepare the Cod Fillets:
    - Pat the cod fillets dry with paper towels.
    - Season both sides of the cod fillets with salt and pepper.
3. Make the Garlic Butter Sauce:
    - In a small bowl, combine melted butter, minced garlic, and fresh lemon juice.
4. Bake the Cod:
    - Place the seasoned cod fillets in a baking dish or on a baking sheet lined with parchment paper.
    - Spoon the garlic butter mixture evenly over the cod fillets.
5. Bake in the Oven:
    - Bake the cod fillets in the preheated oven for 12-15 minutes, or until the fish is opaque and flakes easily with a fork.
6. Serve:
    - Remove the baked cod from the oven and garnish with chopped fresh parsley, if desired.
    - Serve immediately with lemon wedges on the side.

This Baked Cod with Garlic Butter is tender, flavorful, and pairs wonderfully with steamed vegetables, rice, or a fresh salad. It's a simple yet impressive dish that's perfect for both weeknight dinners and special occasions!

Vegan Sloppy Joes

Ingredients:

- 1 cup dried lentils, rinsed and drained
- 3 cups vegetable broth or water
- 1 tablespoon olive oil
- 1 onion, diced
- 1 bell pepper, diced (any color)
- 2 cloves garlic, minced
- 1 can (15 oz) tomato sauce
- 2 tablespoons tomato paste
- 2 tablespoons maple syrup or brown sugar
- 1 tablespoon soy sauce or tamari
- 1 tablespoon apple cider vinegar
- 1 tablespoon chili powder
- 1 teaspoon smoked paprika
- 1/2 teaspoon cumin
- Salt and pepper, to taste
- Hamburger buns or bread of choice, for serving

Instructions:

1. Cook the Lentils:
    - In a medium saucepan, combine the rinsed lentils and vegetable broth or water.
    - Bring to a boil over high heat, then reduce the heat to low, cover, and simmer for 20-25 minutes, or until the lentils are tender and most of the liquid is absorbed. Drain any excess liquid if needed.
2. Prepare the Filling:
    - In a large skillet or frying pan, heat olive oil over medium heat.
    - Add diced onion and bell pepper. Sauté for 5-7 minutes, until softened.
3. Add Garlic and Spices:
    - Add minced garlic, chili powder, smoked paprika, and cumin to the skillet. Cook for 1 minute, stirring constantly, until fragrant.
4. Combine with Sauce:
    - Stir in tomato sauce, tomato paste, maple syrup or brown sugar, soy sauce or tamari, and apple cider vinegar. Mix well to combine.
5. Simmer:
    - Add cooked lentils to the skillet with the sauce mixture.
    - Stir everything together and simmer over low heat for 10-15 minutes, stirring occasionally, to allow the flavors to meld together and the mixture to thicken.
6. Season and Serve:
    - Taste and adjust seasoning with salt and pepper as needed.
7. Assemble and Serve:

- Spoon the vegan sloppy joe mixture onto hamburger buns or bread of your choice.
- Serve hot and enjoy your delicious Vegan Sloppy Joes!

These Vegan Sloppy Joes are flavorful, hearty, and perfect for a family-friendly meal. They're a great way to enjoy a classic comfort food dish in a plant-based version!

Roasted Vegetable and Hummus Wraps

Ingredients:

- 4 large whole wheat or spinach tortillas
- 1 cup hummus (store-bought or homemade)
- 2 cups mixed roasted vegetables (such as bell peppers, zucchini, eggplant, cherry tomatoes)
- 1 cup baby spinach leaves
- 1/2 cup crumbled feta cheese (optional)
- Salt and pepper, to taste
- Fresh herbs (such as parsley or basil), chopped (optional)

Instructions:

1. Prepare the Roasted Vegetables:
    - Preheat your oven to 400°F (200°C).
    - Cut the vegetables into bite-sized pieces and spread them out on a baking sheet.
    - Drizzle with olive oil, season with salt and pepper, and toss to coat.
    - Roast in the preheated oven for 20-25 minutes, or until the vegetables are tender and lightly charred.
2. Assemble the Wraps:
    - Lay out the tortillas on a flat surface.
    - Spread about 1/4 cup of hummus evenly over each tortilla.
3. Add the Roasted Vegetables:
    - Divide the roasted vegetables evenly among the tortillas, spreading them over the hummus.
4. Add Spinach and Cheese (if using):
    - Top each wrap with a handful of baby spinach leaves and a sprinkle of crumbled feta cheese, if desired.
5. Optional: Fresh Herbs:
    - Sprinkle with chopped fresh herbs, such as parsley or basil, for added flavor.
6. Roll Up the Wraps:
    - Fold in the sides of each tortilla, then roll it up tightly from the bottom to enclose the filling.
7. Serve:
    - Slice the wraps in half diagonally, if desired.
    - Serve immediately, or wrap tightly in foil or plastic wrap for a portable lunch option.

These Roasted Vegetable and Hummus Wraps are versatile and can be customized with your favorite vegetables and toppings. They're packed with fiber, vitamins, and protein, making them a nutritious and satisfying meal choice!

Asian Chicken Lettuce Wraps

Ingredients:

- 1 lb (450g) ground chicken (or turkey)
- 1 tablespoon sesame oil
- 2 cloves garlic, minced
- 1 tablespoon fresh ginger, minced
- 1/2 cup onion, finely chopped
- 1/2 cup bell pepper (any color), finely chopped
- 1/4 cup hoisin sauce
- 2 tablespoons soy sauce
- 1 tablespoon rice vinegar
- 1 tablespoon Sriracha sauce (optional, for heat)
- 1/2 cup water chestnuts, chopped
- 1/4 cup green onions, chopped
- Salt and pepper, to taste
- 1 head of butter lettuce or iceberg lettuce, leaves separated and washed

Instructions:

1. Cook the Ground Chicken:
    - Heat sesame oil in a large skillet or wok over medium-high heat.
    - Add minced garlic and ginger, sauté for 1 minute until fragrant.
2. Add Vegetables:
    - Add chopped onion and bell pepper to the skillet. Cook for 3-4 minutes until vegetables are softened.
3. Cook the Chicken:
    - Add ground chicken to the skillet. Cook, breaking up with a spoon, until chicken is browned and cooked through.
4. Make the Sauce:
    - In a small bowl, mix together hoisin sauce, soy sauce, rice vinegar, and Sriracha sauce (if using). Pour the sauce over the chicken mixture in the skillet.
5. Add Water Chestnuts and Green Onions:
    - Stir in chopped water chestnuts and green onions. Cook for another 2-3 minutes until heated through.
    - Season with salt and pepper to taste.
6. Assemble the Lettuce Wraps:
    - Spoon a portion of the chicken mixture into each lettuce leaf.
7. Serve:
    - Arrange the filled lettuce wraps on a platter.
    - Garnish with extra green onions, if desired.
    - Serve immediately and enjoy your delicious Asian Chicken Lettuce Wraps!

These lettuce wraps are light, flavorful, and can be enjoyed as an appetizer or a main dish. They're also customizable—you can add shredded carrots, peanuts, or cilantro for additional texture and flavor. Perfect for a quick and healthy meal!

Stuffed Bell Peppers with Quinoa and Ground Turkey

Ingredients:

- 4 large bell peppers (any color)
- 1 cup quinoa, rinsed
- 1 lb (450g) ground turkey
- 1 tablespoon olive oil
- 1 onion, diced
- 2 cloves garlic, minced
- 1 can (14.5 oz) diced tomatoes, drained
- 1 teaspoon dried oregano
- 1 teaspoon dried basil
- 1/2 teaspoon smoked paprika
- Salt and pepper, to taste
- 1 cup shredded mozzarella cheese (or cheese of choice)
- Fresh parsley or basil, chopped (for garnish, optional)

Instructions:

1. Preheat the Oven:
    - Preheat your oven to 375°F (190°C).
2. Prepare the Bell Peppers:
    - Cut the tops off the bell peppers and remove the seeds and membranes from the inside. Rinse them under cold water and set aside.
3. Cook the Quinoa:
    - In a medium saucepan, bring 2 cups of water to a boil.
    - Add the rinsed quinoa, reduce heat to low, cover, and simmer for about 15 minutes, or until quinoa is cooked and water is absorbed. Remove from heat and fluff with a fork.
4. Prepare the Filling:
    - Heat olive oil in a large skillet over medium heat.
    - Add diced onion and garlic, sauté for 2-3 minutes until softened.
5. Cook the Ground Turkey:
    - Add ground turkey to the skillet. Cook, breaking it up with a spoon, until browned and cooked through.
6. Combine Ingredients:
    - Stir in drained diced tomatoes, dried oregano, dried basil, smoked paprika, salt, and pepper. Cook for another 2-3 minutes to combine flavors.
7. Assemble the Stuffed Peppers:
    - Stir cooked quinoa into the turkey mixture until well combined.
    - Spoon the filling evenly into each prepared bell pepper.
8. Bake:
    - Place the stuffed bell peppers upright in a baking dish.

- Cover with foil and bake in the preheated oven for 30-35 minutes, or until the peppers are tender.
9. Add Cheese and Finish Baking:
    - Remove the foil and sprinkle shredded mozzarella cheese over the tops of the stuffed peppers.
    - Return to the oven and bake uncovered for an additional 5-7 minutes, or until the cheese is melted and bubbly.
10. Serve:
    - Remove from the oven and let cool slightly.
    - Garnish with chopped fresh parsley or basil, if desired.
    - Serve hot and enjoy your delicious Stuffed Bell Peppers with Quinoa and Ground Turkey!

These stuffed peppers are not only nutritious but also packed with flavor from the quinoa, ground turkey, and aromatic herbs. They make for a wholesome meal that's perfect for lunch or dinner!

Lemon Pepper Salmon

Ingredients:

- 4 salmon fillets (about 6 oz each), skin-on or skinless
- 2 tablespoons olive oil
- 2-3 cloves garlic, minced
- Zest of 1 lemon
- Juice of 1 lemon
- 1 teaspoon freshly ground black pepper
- 1/2 teaspoon salt, or to taste
- Fresh parsley, chopped (for garnish)
- Lemon slices (for serving)

Instructions:

1. Preheat the Oven:
    - Preheat your oven to 400°F (200°C).
2. Prepare the Salmon:
    - Pat the salmon fillets dry with paper towels and place them on a baking sheet lined with parchment paper or aluminum foil.
3. Make the Lemon Pepper Marinade:
    - In a small bowl, whisk together olive oil, minced garlic, lemon zest, lemon juice, freshly ground black pepper, and salt.
4. Marinate the Salmon:
    - Brush or spoon the lemon pepper marinade evenly over the salmon fillets, coating both sides.
5. Bake the Salmon:
    - Bake the salmon in the preheated oven for 12-15 minutes, or until the salmon is cooked through and flakes easily with a fork. Cooking time may vary depending on the thickness of your salmon fillets.
6. Serve:
    - Remove the salmon from the oven and let it rest for a few minutes.
    - Garnish with chopped fresh parsley and serve with lemon slices on the side.
7. Optional Grilling Method:
    - Alternatively, you can grill the salmon on a preheated grill over medium-high heat for about 4-5 minutes per side, or until cooked through.
8. Enjoy Your Lemon Pepper Salmon:
    - Serve the lemon pepper salmon hot, accompanied by your favorite sides such as steamed vegetables, rice, or salad.

This Lemon Pepper Salmon recipe is perfect for a quick and healthy dinner option. The combination of lemon, pepper, and garlic enhances the natural flavors of the salmon, making it a delightful dish that's both light and flavorful.

Southwestern Quinoa Salad

Ingredients:

- 1 cup quinoa, rinsed
- 2 cups water or vegetable broth
- 1 can (15 oz) black beans, drained and rinsed
- 1 cup corn kernels (fresh, canned, or frozen)
- 1 red bell pepper, diced
- 1/2 red onion, finely chopped
- 1 jalapeño, seeded and finely chopped (optional, for heat)
- 1/4 cup chopped fresh cilantro
- 1 avocado, diced
- Juice of 2 limes
- 3 tablespoons olive oil
- 1 teaspoon ground cumin
- 1/2 teaspoon chili powder
- Salt and pepper, to taste
- Optional toppings: sliced cherry tomatoes, diced cucumber, crumbled feta cheese, sliced green onions

Instructions:

1. Cook the Quinoa:
    - In a medium saucepan, combine quinoa and water or vegetable broth. Bring to a boil over medium-high heat.
    - Reduce heat to low, cover, and simmer for 15-20 minutes, or until quinoa is cooked and water is absorbed. Remove from heat and let it sit, covered, for 5 minutes. Fluff with a fork and let cool.
2. Prepare the Dressing:
    - In a small bowl, whisk together lime juice, olive oil, ground cumin, chili powder, salt, and pepper.
3. Assemble the Salad:
    - In a large bowl, combine cooked quinoa, black beans, corn kernels, diced red bell pepper, finely chopped red onion, chopped jalapeño (if using), and chopped fresh cilantro.
4. Add the Dressing:
    - Pour the dressing over the quinoa mixture in the bowl. Toss gently to combine, ensuring everything is evenly coated with the dressing.
5. Add Avocado:
    - Gently fold in diced avocado. Be careful not to mash the avocado too much.
6. Chill and Serve:
    - Cover the bowl with plastic wrap and refrigerate the salad for at least 30 minutes to allow the flavors to meld together.
7. Serve:

- Before serving, give the salad a final toss.
- Garnish with additional toppings like sliced cherry tomatoes, diced cucumber, crumbled feta cheese, or sliced green onions, if desired.
- Serve chilled as a delicious and nutritious side dish or a light main course.

This Southwestern Quinoa Salad is packed with protein, fiber, and fresh flavors. It's perfect for picnics, potlucks, or as a satisfying meal prep option. Enjoy the vibrant colors and zesty taste of this delicious salad!

Chicken Enchiladas

Ingredients:

- 1 lb (450g) boneless, skinless chicken breasts or thighs
- Salt and pepper, to taste
- 1 tablespoon olive oil
- 1 small onion, finely chopped
- 2 cloves garlic, minced
- 1 can (15 oz) black beans, drained and rinsed
- 1 can (4 oz) diced green chilies, drained
- 1 teaspoon ground cumin
- 1 teaspoon chili powder
- 1/2 teaspoon paprika
- 1/2 teaspoon dried oregano
- 1/4 teaspoon cayenne pepper (optional, for heat)
- 1 can (10 oz) red enchilada sauce, divided
- 1 cup shredded cheese (cheddar, Monterey Jack, or Mexican blend)
- 8-10 small flour tortillas (6-inch size)
- Chopped fresh cilantro, for garnish
- Sour cream, sliced avocado, or diced tomatoes, for serving (optional)

Instructions:

1. Cook the Chicken:
    - Season chicken breasts or thighs with salt and pepper.
    - In a large skillet or pan, heat olive oil over medium-high heat.
    - Add chicken and cook until golden brown on both sides and cooked through, about 6-7 minutes per side depending on thickness.
    - Remove chicken from skillet and shred using two forks or chop into small pieces.
2. Prepare the Filling:
    - In the same skillet, add chopped onion and garlic. Sauté until softened, about 3-4 minutes.
    - Stir in black beans, diced green chilies, ground cumin, chili powder, paprika, dried oregano, and cayenne pepper (if using).
    - Add shredded chicken back into the skillet and mix well to combine.
    - Stir in about 1/2 cup of the enchilada sauce and half of the shredded cheese. Mix until cheese is melted and everything is evenly coated.
3. Assemble the Enchiladas:
    - Preheat your oven to 375°F (190°C).
    - Pour a small amount of enchilada sauce into the bottom of a baking dish and spread it evenly.
    - Spoon about 1/3 cup of the chicken filling onto each tortilla and roll tightly. Place seam-side down in the baking dish.
4. Bake the Enchiladas:

    - Pour the remaining enchilada sauce over the rolled tortillas, spreading it evenly.
    - Sprinkle the remaining shredded cheese on top.
5. Bake in the Oven:
    - Cover the baking dish with aluminum foil and bake in the preheated oven for 20-25 minutes, or until the enchiladas are heated through and the cheese is melted and bubbly.
6. Serve:
    - Remove from the oven and let cool slightly.
    - Garnish with chopped fresh cilantro.
    - Serve hot with optional toppings such as sour cream, sliced avocado, or diced tomatoes.

These chicken enchiladas are savory, cheesy, and full of delicious Mexican flavors. They're perfect for a family dinner or for entertaining guests. Enjoy the hearty and comforting taste of homemade chicken enchiladas!

Ratatouille

Ingredients:

- 1 eggplant, diced
- 2 zucchinis, diced
- 1 yellow bell pepper, diced
- 1 red bell pepper, diced
- 1 onion, diced
- 3 cloves garlic, minced
- 4 tomatoes, diced (or 1 can, 14 oz diced tomatoes)
- 2 tablespoons tomato paste
- 2 tablespoons olive oil
- 1 teaspoon dried thyme
- 1 teaspoon dried oregano
- Salt and pepper, to taste
- Fresh basil or parsley, chopped (for garnish)

Instructions:

1. Prepare the Vegetables:
    - Dice the eggplant, zucchinis, yellow bell pepper, red bell pepper, onion, and tomatoes into evenly sized pieces.
2. Cook the Ratatouille:
    - In a large skillet or Dutch oven, heat olive oil over medium heat.
    - Add diced onion and cook for 2-3 minutes until softened.
    - Add minced garlic and cook for another 1 minute until fragrant.
3. Add the Vegetables:
    - Add diced eggplant, zucchinis, yellow bell pepper, and red bell pepper to the skillet.
    - Cook, stirring occasionally, for about 10 minutes until vegetables start to soften.
4. Add Tomatoes and Seasonings:
    - Stir in diced tomatoes, tomato paste, dried thyme, dried oregano, salt, and pepper.
    - Mix well to combine all ingredients.
5. Simmer:
    - Reduce heat to low, cover the skillet or Dutch oven with a lid, and simmer for 20-25 minutes, stirring occasionally, until vegetables are tender and flavors have melded together.
6. Adjust Seasoning:
    - Taste and adjust seasoning with salt and pepper as needed.
7. Serve:
    - Remove from heat and garnish with chopped fresh basil or parsley.
8. Enjoy Ratatouille:
    - Serve hot as a side dish or a light main course.

- Ratatouille can be enjoyed on its own, with crusty bread, over rice, or alongside grilled meats.

This Ratatouille recipe is versatile and can be customized with your favorite herbs and vegetables. It's a delightful dish that celebrates the flavors of fresh summer produce in a comforting and satisfying way.

Coconut Curry Chicken

Ingredients:

- 1 lb (450g) boneless, skinless chicken breasts or thighs, cut into bite-sized pieces
- 1 tablespoon vegetable oil or coconut oil
- 1 onion, finely chopped
- 3 cloves garlic, minced
- 1 tablespoon fresh ginger, grated or minced
- 1 red bell pepper, sliced
- 1 yellow bell pepper, sliced
- 1 can (14 oz) coconut milk (full-fat for creamier texture)
- 2 tablespoons red curry paste
- 1 tablespoon curry powder
- 1 tablespoon soy sauce or tamari
- 1 tablespoon brown sugar or coconut sugar (optional, for sweetness)
- Juice of 1 lime
- Salt and pepper, to taste
- Fresh cilantro, chopped (for garnish)
- Cooked rice or naan bread, for serving

Instructions:

1. Cook the Chicken:
    - Heat vegetable oil or coconut oil in a large skillet or pot over medium-high heat.
    - Add chicken pieces and cook until browned on all sides and cooked through. Remove chicken from the skillet and set aside.
2. Prepare the Curry Base:
    - In the same skillet or pot, add chopped onion, minced garlic, and grated ginger. Sauté for 2-3 minutes until fragrant and onions are softened.
3. Add Bell Peppers and Spices:
    - Add sliced red bell pepper and yellow bell pepper to the skillet. Cook for another 3-4 minutes until peppers are slightly softened.
    - Stir in red curry paste and curry powder. Cook for 1 minute, stirring constantly to coat the vegetables with the spices.
4. Simmer with Coconut Milk:
    - Pour in coconut milk and stir well to combine with the spices and vegetables.
    - Bring the mixture to a simmer over medium heat.
5. Add Chicken and Seasonings:
    - Return cooked chicken pieces to the skillet.
    - Add soy sauce or tamari, brown sugar or coconut sugar (if using), and lime juice.
    - Season with salt and pepper to taste. Stir to combine all ingredients.
6. Simmer and Thicken:

- Reduce heat to low and let the curry simmer for 10-15 minutes, stirring occasionally, to allow the flavors to meld together and the sauce to thicken slightly.
7. Serve:
    - Remove from heat and garnish with chopped fresh cilantro.
    - Serve hot over cooked rice or with naan bread on the side.

Enjoy this Coconut Curry Chicken with its creamy coconut milk base and aromatic curry spices. It's a comforting and satisfying dish that pairs perfectly with rice or naan for a complete meal.

Mediterranean Stuffed Sweet Potatoes

Ingredients:

- 4 medium sweet potatoes
- 1 tablespoon olive oil
- 1 can (15 oz) chickpeas, drained and rinsed
- 1 cup cherry tomatoes, halved
- 1/2 English cucumber, diced
- 1/4 cup red onion, finely chopped
- 1/4 cup Kalamata olives, sliced
- 1/4 cup crumbled feta cheese (optional)
- Juice of 1 lemon
- 2 tablespoons chopped fresh parsley
- Salt and pepper, to taste
- Greek yogurt or tzatziki sauce, for serving (optional)

Instructions:

1. Prepare the Sweet Potatoes:
    - Preheat your oven to 400°F (200°C).
    - Scrub the sweet potatoes clean and pierce each one several times with a fork.
    - Rub sweet potatoes with olive oil and sprinkle with salt. Place them on a baking sheet lined with parchment paper.
2. Roast the Sweet Potatoes:
    - Roast sweet potatoes in the preheated oven for 45-60 minutes, or until tender and easily pierced with a fork.
3. Prepare the Filling:
    - In a large bowl, combine drained and rinsed chickpeas, halved cherry tomatoes, diced cucumber, finely chopped red onion, sliced Kalamata olives, crumbled feta cheese (if using), lemon juice, and chopped fresh parsley.
    - Season with salt and pepper to taste. Toss everything together gently to combine.
4. Assemble the Stuffed Sweet Potatoes:
    - Once sweet potatoes are roasted and tender, slice each one lengthwise and slightly mash the flesh with a fork to create a pocket.
    - Spoon the Mediterranean filling mixture generously into each sweet potato.
5. Serve:
    - Serve stuffed sweet potatoes warm, garnished with additional fresh parsley and a dollop of Greek yogurt or tzatziki sauce, if desired.

These Mediterranean Stuffed Sweet Potatoes are packed with fresh flavors, protein from chickpeas, and healthy fats from olives and optional feta cheese. They make for a satisfying and wholesome meal that's perfect for lunch or dinner!

Beef and Mushroom Stir-Fry

Ingredients:

- 1 lb (450g) beef steak (flank steak or sirloin), thinly sliced against the grain
- 2 tablespoons soy sauce
- 1 tablespoon oyster sauce
- 1 tablespoon hoisin sauce
- 1 tablespoon cornstarch
- 2 tablespoons vegetable oil, divided
- 8 oz (225g) mushrooms (button or cremini), sliced
- 1 onion, thinly sliced
- 3 cloves garlic, minced
- 1 tablespoon fresh ginger, minced
- 1 bell pepper (any color), thinly sliced
- 1 cup broccoli florets
- Salt and pepper, to taste
- Cooked rice or noodles, for serving
- Sesame seeds and chopped green onions, for garnish (optional)

Instructions:

1. Prepare the Beef:
   - In a bowl, combine thinly sliced beef with soy sauce, oyster sauce, hoisin sauce, and cornstarch. Mix well and let it marinate for at least 15-20 minutes.
2. Stir-Fry the Vegetables:
   - Heat 1 tablespoon of vegetable oil in a large skillet or wok over medium-high heat.
   - Add sliced mushrooms and cook for 3-4 minutes until they release their juices and start to brown. Remove mushrooms from the skillet and set aside.
3. Cook the Beef:
   - In the same skillet or wok, add the remaining 1 tablespoon of vegetable oil.
   - Add marinated beef slices in a single layer and cook for 1-2 minutes per side until browned and cooked through. Remove beef from the skillet and set aside.
4. Saute Aromatics and Vegetables:
   - Add thinly sliced onion to the skillet and cook for 2-3 minutes until softened.
   - Stir in minced garlic and minced ginger, cook for 1 minute until fragrant.
5. Combine and Stir-Fry:
   - Add sliced bell pepper and broccoli florets to the skillet. Cook for 3-4 minutes until vegetables are tender-crisp.
6. Combine Beef and Mushrooms:
   - Return cooked mushrooms and beef to the skillet. Stir everything together to combine.
7. Season and Serve:
   - Season the stir-fry with salt and pepper to taste.
   - Serve hot over cooked rice or noodles.
   - Garnish with sesame seeds and chopped green onions, if desired.

Enjoy this Beef and Mushroom Stir-Fry for a flavorful and satisfying meal that's perfect for busy weeknights. Adjust the vegetables and seasonings according to your taste preferences for a personalized stir-fry experience!

Shrimp Tacos with Mango Salsa

Ingredients:

For Shrimp:

- 1 lb (450g) large shrimp, peeled and deveined
- 1 tablespoon olive oil
- 1 teaspoon chili powder
- 1/2 teaspoon cumin
- 1/2 teaspoon paprika
- Salt and pepper, to taste
- Juice of 1 lime

For Mango Salsa:

- 1 ripe mango, peeled and diced
- 1/2 red bell pepper, diced
- 1/4 cup red onion, finely chopped
- 1/4 cup fresh cilantro, chopped
- Juice of 1 lime
- Salt and pepper, to taste

For Tacos:

- 8-10 small flour or corn tortillas
- Shredded cabbage or lettuce
- Avocado slices
- Sour cream or Greek yogurt (optional)
- Lime wedges, for serving

Instructions:

1. Prepare the Mango Salsa:
    - In a bowl, combine diced mango, diced red bell pepper, finely chopped red onion, chopped fresh cilantro, lime juice, salt, and pepper. Mix well and set aside to let the flavors meld.
2. Prepare the Shrimp:
    - In a separate bowl, toss peeled and deveined shrimp with olive oil, chili powder, cumin, paprika, salt, pepper, and lime juice. Ensure shrimp are evenly coated with spices.
3. Cook the Shrimp:
    - Heat a large skillet or grill pan over medium-high heat.
    - Add seasoned shrimp to the skillet and cook for 2-3 minutes per side, until shrimp are pink and opaque. Be careful not to overcook.
4. Warm the Tortillas:
    - While the shrimp are cooking, warm the tortillas in a separate skillet or oven until they are soft and pliable.
5. Assemble the Tacos:

- To assemble each taco, place a spoonful of shredded cabbage or lettuce on a tortilla.
        - Top with cooked shrimp, a spoonful of mango salsa, avocado slices, and a dollop of sour cream or Greek yogurt, if desired.
        - Squeeze fresh lime juice over the taco.
6. Serve:
        - Serve Shrimp Tacos with Mango Salsa immediately, with extra lime wedges on the side.

These Shrimp Tacos with Mango Salsa are bursting with vibrant flavors and textures. They make for a perfect light meal or a delightful option for entertaining guests. Enjoy the combination of sweet mango salsa with spicy shrimp in every bite!

Italian Sausage and Peppers

Ingredients:

- 1 lb (450g) Italian sausage (sweet or spicy), cut into 1-inch pieces
- 2 tablespoons olive oil
- 2 bell peppers (any color), thinly sliced
- 1 large onion, thinly sliced
- 3 cloves garlic, minced
- 1 can (14 oz) diced tomatoes
- 1 can (8 oz) tomato sauce
- 1 teaspoon dried oregano
- 1 teaspoon dried basil
- 1/2 teaspoon red pepper flakes (optional, for heat)
- Salt and pepper, to taste
- Fresh parsley, chopped (for garnish)
- Cooked pasta, rice, or crusty bread, for serving

Instructions:

1. Brown the Sausage:
   - Heat olive oil in a large skillet or Dutch oven over medium-high heat.
   - Add Italian sausage pieces and cook until browned on all sides, about 5-7 minutes. Remove sausage from skillet and set aside.
2. Saute the Vegetables:
   - In the same skillet, add sliced bell peppers and onion. Cook for 5-6 minutes until softened and slightly caramelized.
3. Add Garlic and Tomatoes:
   - Stir in minced garlic and cook for 1 minute until fragrant.
   - Add diced tomatoes (with juices) and tomato sauce to the skillet. Stir to combine.
4. Season and Simmer:
   - Add dried oregano, dried basil, red pepper flakes (if using), salt, and pepper to taste.
   - Return browned sausage pieces to the skillet and stir to combine everything.
5. Simmer the Dish:
   - Reduce heat to low, cover the skillet, and simmer for 20-25 minutes, stirring occasionally, to allow flavors to meld together and sauce to thicken slightly.
6. Serve:
   - Remove from heat and garnish with chopped fresh parsley.
   - Serve Italian Sausage and Peppers hot over cooked pasta, rice, or with crusty bread on the side.

This Italian Sausage and Peppers dish is hearty, flavorful, and perfect for a comforting family meal. The combination of tender sausage, sweet bell peppers, and savory tomato sauce makes it a classic favorite that's easy to prepare and enjoy!

Cauliflower Tikka Masala

Ingredients:

For the Cauliflower:

- 1 large head cauliflower, cut into florets
- 2 tablespoons olive oil
- 1 teaspoon ground cumin
- 1 teaspoon ground coriander
- 1/2 teaspoon turmeric powder
- 1/2 teaspoon paprika
- Salt and pepper, to taste

For the Tikka Masala Sauce:

- 2 tablespoons vegetable oil or ghee
- 1 onion, finely chopped
- 3 cloves garlic, minced
- 1 tablespoon fresh ginger, minced
- 1 can (14 oz) diced tomatoes
- 1 can (14 oz) coconut milk (full-fat for creamier texture)
- 2 teaspoons ground cumin
- 2 teaspoons ground coriander
- 1 teaspoon turmeric powder
- 1 teaspoon paprika
- 1/2 teaspoon cinnamon
- 1/4 teaspoon cayenne pepper (adjust to taste)
- Salt and pepper, to taste
- Fresh cilantro, chopped (for garnish)
- Cooked rice or naan bread, for serving

Instructions:

1. Roast the Cauliflower:
   - Preheat your oven to 400°F (200°C).
   - In a large bowl, toss cauliflower florets with olive oil, ground cumin, ground coriander, turmeric powder, paprika, salt, and pepper until evenly coated.
   - Spread cauliflower florets in a single layer on a baking sheet lined with parchment paper.
   - Roast in the preheated oven for 20-25 minutes, or until cauliflower is tender and slightly caramelized. Remove from oven and set aside.
2. Prepare the Tikka Masala Sauce:
   - Heat vegetable oil or ghee in a large skillet or Dutch oven over medium heat.
   - Add finely chopped onion and sauté for 5-6 minutes until softened and translucent.
   - Stir in minced garlic and minced ginger, and cook for 1-2 minutes until fragrant.
3. Make the Sauce:

- Add diced tomatoes (with juices) to the skillet. Cook for 5-6 minutes, stirring occasionally, until tomatoes break down and release their juices.
- Stir in coconut milk, ground cumin, ground coriander, turmeric powder, paprika, cinnamon, cayenne pepper, salt, and pepper. Mix well to combine all ingredients.

4. **Simmer the Sauce:**
   - Bring the sauce to a simmer over medium heat. Reduce heat to low and let it simmer gently for 10-15 minutes, stirring occasionally, to allow flavors to meld together and sauce to thicken slightly.
5. **Combine Cauliflower and Sauce:**
   - Add roasted cauliflower florets to the skillet with the tikka masala sauce. Stir gently to coat the cauliflower evenly with the sauce.
6. **Serve:**
   - Remove from heat and garnish with chopped fresh cilantro.
   - Serve Cauliflower Tikka Masala hot over cooked rice or with naan bread on the side.

This Cauliflower Tikka Masala is rich, creamy, and packed with aromatic spices. It's a satisfying vegetarian dish that's perfect for a cozy dinner at home. Enjoy the bold flavors and tender cauliflower in every bite!

Greek Salad with Grilled Chicken

Ingredients:

For Grilled Chicken:

- 1 lb (450g) chicken breasts, boneless and skinless
- 2 tablespoons olive oil
- Juice of 1 lemon
- 2 cloves garlic, minced
- 1 teaspoon dried oregano
- Salt and pepper, to taste

For Greek Salad:

- 1 cucumber, diced
- 1 bell pepper (any color), diced
- 1 cup cherry tomatoes, halved
- 1/2 red onion, thinly sliced
- 1/2 cup Kalamata olives, pitted and sliced
- 1/2 cup crumbled feta cheese
- Fresh parsley or oregano, chopped (for garnish)

For Greek Dressing:

- 1/4 cup extra virgin olive oil
- 2 tablespoons red wine vinegar
- 1 teaspoon Dijon mustard
- 1 teaspoon dried oregano
- 1 clove garlic, minced
- Salt and pepper, to taste

Instructions:

1. Marinate and Grill the Chicken:
    - In a bowl or resealable bag, combine olive oil, lemon juice, minced garlic, dried oregano, salt, and pepper.
    - Add chicken breasts to the marinade and coat evenly. Marinate for at least 30 minutes, or up to 4 hours in the refrigerator.
    - Preheat grill or grill pan over medium-high heat. Grill chicken for 6-7 minutes per side, or until fully cooked and internal temperature reaches 165°F (74°C). Remove from grill and let rest for a few minutes before slicing.
2. Prepare Greek Salad:
    - In a large bowl, combine diced cucumber, diced bell pepper, halved cherry tomatoes, thinly sliced red onion, sliced Kalamata olives, and crumbled feta cheese.
3. Make Greek Dressing:
    - In a small bowl, whisk together extra virgin olive oil, red wine vinegar, Dijon mustard, dried oregano, minced garlic, salt, and pepper until well combined.

4. Assemble the Salad:
    - Add sliced grilled chicken to the bowl with the Greek salad ingredients.
    - Drizzle Greek dressing over the salad and gently toss to combine, ensuring everything is evenly coated with dressing.
5. Serve:
    - Garnish Greek Salad with Grilled Chicken with chopped fresh parsley or oregano.
    - Serve immediately, and enjoy this fresh and flavorful Mediterranean-inspired dish!

This Greek Salad with Grilled Chicken is perfect for a light and satisfying meal. It's packed with fresh vegetables, protein-rich grilled chicken, and a tangy Greek dressing that brings all the flavors together. Serve it as a main course salad for lunch or dinner, and enjoy the delicious combination of ingredients!